The
Lofton 6

A Travesty of Justice

DARRYL G. LOFTON

TABLE OF CONTENTS

ACKNOWLEDGMENT

I hope my research clears everything up. Although, my under-standing strengthened after reading Steven Lofton's book: *The Hidden Dimension: An Inside View on the Reality of the Inner City African America.*

Steven and Mom, thanks for outlining your books to form a stepping stone for the point of view shared in this book.

Mom, after reading your book, *Theft by Court*, where you explained the use of codes when enacting law through the court system, I saw that the book was an example of your experience in case number 895188. Initially, I did not understand how it related to our case. You described how judicial systems are designed with codes to impede fair treatment, "enforcing black code." It helped me fully understand what was going on when I was doing my research for this book.

Thank you, family, for surviving, telling your story, and having patience with me as I worked through understanding and writing about our ordeal.

Thank you, my friends and loved ones, for your patience and tolerance. I will try my best to give a thorough and accurate depiction of the time and space in America during this journey.

Index of people:

1. Parents: Leon E. Lofton Jr. and Esther M. Lofton.

2. Siblings: Michael Lofton, Steven Lofton, Verna Lofton, Darryl Lofton, Tracy Lofton, and Nina Lofton (The first six children).

3. Two younger siblings who came later: Gena Lofton and Heather Lofton.

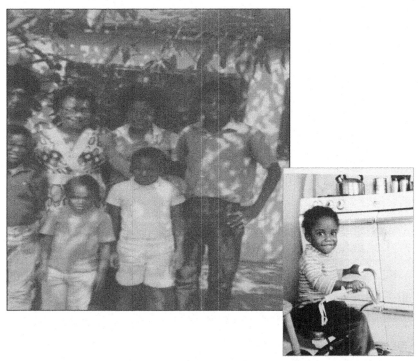

Top row: Steven B. Lofton, Aunt Mary Harris, Verna G. Lofton, Michael L. Lofton, Front row: Darryl G. Lofton, Gena A. Lofton, Tracy L. Lofton. All but Aunt Mary Harris and Gena A. Lofton were part of the Lofton 6.
Inset: Nina Lofton (Lofton 6)

INTRODUCTION

Dates are important. I was reviewing the events that transpired between 1954-1968, which were the years of the Civil Rights Movement, and realized I was not viewing those events in chronological order, or putting them in proper perspective. After brief discussion with different people, I saw that the historical order of laws and their consequences were getting lost in translation. We need a different approach to set the tone of the period (1954-1968), starting with the decision rendered and the fallout of Brown vs. Board of Education (1954). How were lives affected? What happened to the children displaced during these years?

People tend to ask the following questions: "Didn't the Brown ruling make things better?" "Did it end 'Separate but Equal?'" "Didn't it end Jim Crow?" "Did black Americans feel equal after this ruling?" No. They needed marches, sit-ins, squatters, and police beatings to pass a Civil Rights Act in 1964 and a Voting Rights Act in 1965.

Getting the courts to try a case was impossible. Those reasons alone make Brown vs. Board of Education a slave joke. Sequencing must not be overlooked. When our family was torn apart, the Civil Rights Movement was in motion, and in 1964 The Civil Rights

Act was passed, then in 1965 the Voting Rights Act was passed and the result to my family was a firestorm that had erupted.

My family's struggle was the catalyst that formed my journey and now provides a history lesson to all. We were six siblings, hence *The Lofton 6,* the first time we were stripped of our Constitutional rights. Due to the court's collusion and manifest abuse of the laws on the books, my parents were fraudulently denied the right to work. Without due process and equal protection by the law, they were pronounced guilty. Dates matter because they provide a timeline of the hostilities and personalities of indifference during a period of American history when things were unfair and created damages beyond repair. During the Civil Rights Era (1954-1977), our judicial system was at the center of this dysfunction. Below, I have numbered the issues that shaped the foundation of the ideology that defecated on my entire family. Before 1967, cases involving Blacks or Negros were not given the same respect and dignity allotted to those involving other Americans. Most times, many blacks could not get an attorney unless the black person wanted to file their case under discrimination violations (using test cases), which usually fell to a stalemate. Case #895188 involved a civil rights violation which depended entirely on the due process and equal protection clauses that the Civil Rights Act and the Voting Rights Act were supposed to protect. Most cases before these Acts were thrown out or redirected and never made it to a judge, except for occasionally testing the court with trial situations (test cases) or in cases involving a person's death.

Why did my parents wait until 1967 to file a lawsuit resulting in case #895188? First, they did not wait. It would not be until the passing of the Civil Rights Act and the Voting Rights Act that crimes already committed against them magnified their disenfranchisement.

Please keep in mind that ours is but one story when it came to injustices endured by Americans. There are millions more, and I wrote this book to be a voice for them, as well.

Chapter 1

My story begins on June 13, 1961, at a terrible time in American history, when Kennedy was president. I've witnessed eleven presidents, Jim Crow, separate but equal, Brown vs. Board of Education, Civil Rights Acts, Voting Rights Acts, protesting, discrimination, major riots, and I am also the last of the baby boomers.

From 1964 until it became legally permissive for Leon E. Lofton Jr. and Esther M. Lofton to file a lawsuit on April 12, 1967, the Lofton 6 had already been put into foster care, molested, beaten, and thrown into juvenile facilities. In addition, our parents were falsely criminalized, falsely placed, and marked with a strong emphasis towards their criminality.

I understand how this can make a person angry at political and criminal justice systems and the country as a whole. I include country because the picture became more devastating and racially-based when these injustices were deliberately committed against an African American or Negro, or Black man, after being drafted, fighting in Northern Africa and Italy during WWII, and then honorably discharged with a Purple Heart, as was the case for Sergeant Leon E. Lofton Jr. of the US Army.

At the center of my journey:

1. In 1954, the landmark ruling of Brown vs. Board of Education was meant to end racial discrimination. The Brown decision, in large part, was the catalyst for the Civil Rights Movement. When Professor of Education Charles C. Jackson wrote an article in *The Western Journal of Black Studies*, Vol. 31, No. 2, (2007) entitled *The Brown Decision in Retrospect: Commemoration or Celebration* that it was no longer legal to segregate children in school solely their skin color, thereby rejecting the underlying premise that black, brown, red, and yellow meant inferior, he added that it took many years for a considerable number of school districts in the south to even attempt to dismantle their dual school systems.

   Southern California had its way of integrating children of color into the school system. My very first step into a school was after my family was torn apart, and my parents were denied the right to teach or work in the State of California. It should be noted that African American communities did suffer extreme social and economic loss as a result of desegregation. A significant number of the professional and leadership class were educators, administrators, and school counselors, and many of the teachers my parents would speak about lost their jobs. The Los Angeles County School Board offered the lucky teachers less meaningful jobs as substitutes, and the unlucky teachers never got hired. The tactics to obstruct employment of individuals was through fraud and manipulation within the Los Angeles County School Board, with the justice system being complicit in it all.

2. The Civil Rights Act of 1964 was a landmark decision in civil rights and U.S. labor law that outlaws discrimination based on race, color, sex, religion, or national origin. It prohibits unequal application of voter registration requirements, as well as racial segregation in schools, employment, and public accommodations.

3. The Voting Rights Act of 1965 marks the decision to enforce the Fifteenth Amendment of the United States Constitution. It prohibits racial discrimination in voting.

4. Leon E. Lofton Jr. and Esther M. Lofton vs. The Los Angeles Unified School District, Case #895188. On April 12, 1967, my parents believed they needed immediate court action because their children's lives were at stake. However, my mother did not want to waste time on test cases (a test case is a case that would be tested with a mock trial to see if it would not humiliate the court). On May 17, 1954, the United States Supreme Court arrived at a decision that had immediate repercussions on our lives.

Chapter 2

Peacefully But Not Voluntarily

In 1964, the Lofton 6 were set to become wards of the court under a criminal justice system that persecuted black people without any form of due process or equal protection under the law. I coined the term *Lofton 6* in my brain when I was four. I remember it being discussed around the squad cars when the police first busted into my family home, threw my father to the ground, and put him in handcuffs. I also saw the police grabbing my mother and pulling her away crying, and it seemed as if her lips were moving, saying words to ease the tension. I remember a black boot smashing the brand-new fire truck that I had just received for Christmas. I also recall the long walk that evening to a police station to pick up our father and then all of us heading to the church to seek refuge and warmth, eventually falling asleep on the lobby floor after sharing a Bologna sandwich. During the arrest I had heard someone refer to us as "the six children." The six children were transported in different vehicles, and my sister Tracy and I rode together. The Lofton 6 were transported to the rotunda of McClaren Hall which was once located in El Monte, California, a city southeast of Los Angeles, California. For several days, it was more of a home than anywhere the government could have placed me, and certainly more than my family could have provided.

We stood in the middle of the rotunda, a central place in a building with five hallways called "wings," which looked like spokes on a bicycle. The announcement speakers and the vehicle's radios kept referring to us as the Lofton 6. The Lofton 6 remains in my head also because every time we were rounded up for the court, we were referenced as the Lofton 6. Even a Los Angeles Times article in 1972 read:

"*A family of 8 Arrested in Eviction Protest* reported by Associated Press. Eight members of a family troubled for years by unemployment and dislocation were arrested on Wednesday after they refused to leave a Los Angeles courthouse where they were trying to fight an eviction order. Police said that the family has a history of squatting, dating back at least to 1965 when they moved their belongings into the Los Angeles police headquarters. A charitable organization had placed Leon, Esther Lofton, and six of their children at the downtown Dark Hotel last Dec. 15, according to the hotel's manager, Paul Clement. After the organization refused to support them further, said Clement, the family said they were unable to pay rent but declined to leave. The hotel obtained a court order, and the sheriff's deputies arrived on Tuesday to carry out the order. Clement said that the family left 'peacefully but not voluntarily.' On Wednesday morning, the family trooped into the County Courthouse and demanded to see the presiding judge, said police. Superior Court Judge, William Hogoboom, told them that they could appeal the eviction order but that he could not 'set aside a judgment just on someone walking into the courtroom.' When they refused to leave the courthouse, said a police spokesman, 10 officers took them into custody."

Who were Leon and Esther? When they left Baltimore, MD, for a better future and better prospects for teaching jobs, they packed up the three kids and headed west before the ruling of Brown vs. Board of Education (1954). In my brother's book, *The Hidden Dimension: An inside view on the reality of the inner city African American,* he explains how the family traveled around in a big blue station wagon we called "big blue goose."

My parents were teachers, but bureaucratic manipulation and fraudulent acts and atrocities by the state kept them unemployed in California. How? One way was by refusing to accept their teaching credentials. California also had a test requirement that set people up for failure. My father was not allowed to take it, and my mother was never going to pass it. As my mother Esther M. Lofton explains, she received her teaching certificate from Coppin College for girls in Virginia but according to the Board of Education in California, she wasn't qualified to teach. Apart from this, being arrested and jailed didn't help matters.

Meanwhile, my dad, Leon E. Lofton Jr.., received his teaching degree from West Virginia University. They met back in Baltimore through my dad's little sister, Aunt Rosemary Tyler. Leon was a WWII Purple Heart recipient and a staunch believer in "The Rule of Law." I will honestly admit, that I have never seen a man love a woman and a woman love a man like my folks loved each other. The two of them stood up against everything that was against them (friends, family, or foes).

My brother explained in his book how great it was to have our parents as teachers when he was little. He also described how I came about in their travels from California while heading north looking for work. I was born in Anchorage, Alaska where my father was trying to find a job. Each morning he left the house to look for work. Other times he left to pound the pavement while carrying a sign that read, 'Can anyone help family and me back to California?' This was how dismal our situation was.

Carrying signs sometimes led to good things. When the blue goose broke down somewhere between Seattle and Anchorage, a nice German-American gentleman who had also fought in WWII (albeit for the other side) saw our situation, he helped tow us from the side of the road to a small town just outside of Anchorage. This good Samaritan and my parents became good friends, and later advised my father that instead of carrying a sign in Anchorage he should seek work in King Cove, Alaska because there were two 2-year government teaching jobs that were open. This was great news and allowed my parents to work for a full year and save enough money to make another go of it in California.

Once back in Los Angeles, things began to really unravel. My sister, Tracy, was born in 1962 in L.A. just as my parents were being stripped of their rights, according to my mother. This is where we saw the real fallout of Brown vs. The Board of Education. The courts were not sympathetic to black people in general during this time, and it wasn't even until 1964 when the Civil Rights Act was revised and the Voting Rights Act passed in 1965. Earlier, I wrote that my parents felt the urgency because children's lives were at stake. Before my parents could legally file a lawsuit, the state had already broken up my family and labeled my parents as infamous villains.

In 1967 when the dust settled amid all the chaos, and after the passing of the Civil Rights Act in 1964, Leon and Esther filed their civil case against the Los Angeles County School Board, in the Superior Court in the County of Los Angeles. The delay was due to the racial components in the system of law and justice. Two promises were broken: first, that Leon, a schoolteacher before being drafted into WWII, would return to a teaching position upon fulfilling military duties, and second, that both Leon and Esther could be schoolteachers. Esther was a grade school teacher, and Leon was a vice principal in south Los Angeles. They bought a home and were teaching under contract with the Los Angeles County School Board before the Breach of Contract.

The nature of their case was a conspiracy to deprive Leon and Esther of their right to work. Through fraud and political maneuvers (Dad always added something he called "manifest and abuse"), bureaucracies manipulated the system to hand out false charges – vagrancy, unwillingness to provide for the family – to hinder my parents.

Their documents were misplaced or destroyed after a forced violent intrusion on their home by law enforcement in violation of the 4th Amendment, which forbids having the police force committing illegal searches and seizures. Their right to due process was infringed upon because the search occurred before there were any charges or warrants. Unfair judicial decisions followed and went unchallenged because essential witnesses were denied access or intimidated to prevent them from coming forward. During the home invasions without warrants, the police searched their furniture and seized their mail.

From 1964 through the next twenty-plus years, they received governmental shaming and labeling with egregious patterns of intent. Later in life, my parents found some joy participating in the Veterans of Foreign Wars (VFW), but that wasn't enough to offset all that they had endured. These actions would go on for several years until all six of their children (which later increased to eight) would reach the age of eighteen and be released from an institution or foster home. Some of us were released because our parents consented to keep the kids in school, especially the two youngest: Gena and Heather Lofton. But even the two youngest would experience institutions and foster homes for years until released under strict conditions.

Leon and Esther were never convicted of any crime. They believed that a black criminal would have a harder time standing up for their rights and receiving due process. Although their experience of harassment went on for well over thirty years, they would say that the Constitution was the most important document to an American citizen. At times, we lived as homeless people in downtown Los Angeles, and for many years while we were in various institutions, Dad, Mom, Mike, and Verna even lived in a car. Steve was living on his own, but everyone always managed to pull themselves together to pursue justice.

Sometimes, when the family reunited between foster home placements or during institutional release, all the children accompanied our parents and marched in downtown Englewood, California, carrying picket signs we made as colorful as possible so they would stand out, which read, "School Teachers Denied the Right to Work" or "Citizens Denied Due Process," and once again arrests would be the end result. This became a way of life for two people and their children who only wanted better teaching facilities for students and their teaching careers restored. Dad always spoke of the family unit. We were a family unit whether we were together or apart.

I grew up knowing my father as a military man. We were all reminded quite regularly that Leon was a Master Sergeant, that he

Leon and Esther Lofton

fought in North Africa and Italy, and that he was awarded a Purple Heart for the wounds he suffered. He was known for giving long, drawn-out lectures and sometimes delivering a blow to the side of the head if he felt you did not understand him or agree with him. He usually spoke to us children with authority. He enjoyed being in charge. My mother respected him like he was the President of the United States. She really loved my father.

So far, I have introduced my family to you. I told you about my mother and father's troubles after the ruling in Brown vs. Board of Education, which led to the breakup of my family, and how we children had to go to foster homes when they were incarcerated. After we six children were taken following our parents' arrest, removed from our home in south-central Los Angeles, and watched my toy firetruck trampled by the police as my father was thrown to the ground and handcuffed, McClaren Hall became my introduction to state institutions.

From McClaren Hall we dispersed to foster homes where Tracy and I were eventually molested. When we became too old for foster homes, I was sent to boys' homes or juvenile hall. The next time I saw my dad, he had aged and sported a grey beard. My mother showed signs of age as well but was still pretty.

Chapter 3

McClaren Hall and the Rotunda

There we were, the 6 of us (Michael age 10, Steven age 8, Verna age 7, I was age 4, Tracy age 3, and Nina two-months old) standing in the center of the rotunda of McClaren Hall in March 1966. It was a place for children, similar to a juvenile hall, but most children are usually placed in foster care because they've suffered domestic violence or family problems that were deemed non-criminal.

We were transported here when our parents were first hauled off to jail. Standing in the center, the place had an eerie quality, especially down the five dark tunnel hallways. The building resembled a wagon wheel, with each hallway a wooden spoke and the central cog the hall where we stood, shivering and scared. Loudly over the microphone, we heard an announcement about the arrival of Lofton 6.

Of the six of us, Michael was the eldest, and Steven was next. A male counselor escorted them down a hallway. A nurse took away Nina, who was only two months old, down to the nursery and infirmary wing. Verna and Tracy were taken along with some ladies to get fitted for clothing and bedding. I was the only one left standing all alone, four years old, in a new and scary place. A man came and got me, and we walked down a hallway. I remember asking for Tracy, but he did not respond.

I changed into a t-shirt, blue jeans, and a pair of baby shoes. Tracy joined me later, with the other little kids of our age. For the children of ages four, five, and six, the jeans, t-shirt, and sneakers were the standard dress. I believe the dress code was because people escaped or ran away a lot, but I could never understand why people left because it was the most fabulous place ever. I was serving time and loving it.

The counselor and I walked to a dorm room, which was a huge bay area. Two double doors opened to a big room with several bunk beds. Walking through there, the structure seemed old with several layers of white paint on the walls. On the windows, there were thick, octagon-wired screens tied together that resembled the chicken wire fence on a chicken coop, only with thicker webbing. Boys were in one open bay room, and through another double-sized door in the center were Tracy and the girls. We said hi, and I went to play with the little boys while she went to play with the little girls.

The photo on the next page is of McClaren Hall and its circular rotunda, where the six of us children were first delivered in 1966.

We had fun the first night. There were probably 30 kids all together in the wing with Tracy and me. We soon realized that children arrived and were released all the time, usually in the morning after court. As they waited, children played with toy cars, trucks, games like Candy Land and Parcheesi, balls, and things to ride on. There were several nurses and counselors. We all got

The rotunda at old McClaren Hall.

ready for bed by nine o'clock. But wait, that was not all. We always had a bedtime snack – some milk and a couple of honey-graham crackers – while at McClaren Hall, up until my last visit at age 15. I loved the graham crackers.

Our only request was that they keep Tracy and me together. Every week, people viewed the children. We got into this glass viewing box for prospective foster parents or adoptive parents to look at us. This only happened a couple of times because concerned citizens always complained and asked to change this practice, and I think these folks were watching out for us. They would walk by, looking at us like the Magilla Gorilla cartoon. I recall once when a kid hollered, "Mommy how much is that gorilla in the window?" This continued for several weeks. Every week, the people only wanted me, the boy. It was getting almost impossible to place Tracy and me together. We were also beginning to really like it there. Later on, some of the skills I learned while in McClaren Hall would aid in protecting myself from bullies. A couple of skirmishes I had were over the way I rocked myself to sleep. Everyone advised me to stop rocking. I would not, especially in McClaren Hall. Why? Because no one humped my backside when I rocked myself continuously from side-to-side in order to fall asleep. Food was good, the school was fun, and we played with many children every day. It was hard to go, but the time came. The very first foster home and they only took me. Tracy had to go to another foster home.

Chapter 4

The Shaw Foster Home Circling the Pole

Mr. and Mrs. Shaw were a lovely Caucasian couple with a special needs son. Away from my family, I was in my first foster home without even my little sister Tracy to watch over. No seeing little new baby sister Nina. No bigger sister, Verna, who we used to call Gail (her middle name) because we already had an Aunt Verna. I was indeed very sad here. I cried a lot. I did not know anyone, and right out of the starting block, I would be in the middle of a controversy, a black boy in a white foster home.

Was this conducive to the development of a black child? I was at the center of every discussion. Jobs in the country were systematically racially divided. How? I was in the system because my parents could not get gainful employment in their desired and trained positions as trained educators. The black social workers felt slighted because they did not want to get cut out of placing a black child in a black foster home. I will explain how the black social workers put Tracy and I anywhere that they could. Most places were abusive and took me in to make ends meet. I have learned from our American history not to dwell on black self-hate because we as a race were still evolving. It was the 60s and 70s, with racial, sexual, and financial tension everywhere. I've seen so many issues resolve to skin color when what should matter in this country is the rule of law. Then again, the law is not always fair to people of color, anyway. Personally, the Shaw foster care was the best foster home that I was ever in.

I was in a good school and speaking articulately for a 4-year old. "He's so articulate," I would hear adults say. I had some of the best cookies. I heard of and ate a macaroon cookie for the first time at the Shaw foster care. Not the ones with the fake-coconut shavings that everyone thinks are real; I preferred the pure cookie crunching without the coconut. They were very delicious to me. I had nice clothes to wear.

The couple had a son; I think his name was Michael, but my stay was so brief and such a long time ago that I'm not sure. However, their son was mentally challenged, and my only duty was to play with him but, do not stop his path. This was not a real duty because I enjoyed helping him get better. He spent most of his day walking around a pole in the backyard, a tether ball pole but with no rope or ball attached. Well, the boy circled that pole for several hours every day, from the morning after breakfast till nap time. He would get up and go outside without saying a word to anyone. It was like the movie *Midnight Express* where the American drug smuggler was sentenced to a Turkish prison. In that prison, the inmates walked in a counter clock-wise direction all day long. That was what Mr. & Mrs. Shaw's son did all day.

Was I only being used to provide medical companionship services for their son? I did not think so, and I still don't. The parents were hoping that with me, their son might come out of his disorder. I talked to him and tried to make him laugh, but often failed.

He was older than me, just small for his age. I was four years old but almost his size, possibly skinnier.

I sometimes walked around the pole with him, but it got boring. The parents saw that we were getting closer. Michael Shaw started to play chase games with me and broke himself away from circling that pole. But good things eventually come to an end. The controversy was heating up vigorously, and at 4 years old, I understood that the discussions between the white foster parent and the black social worker were about black children needing to be in black foster homes. Before I take you to my first foster care home with Tracy, let me explain what a black foster parent was like in those days.

Chapter 5

Thorn of Rose Bush Meets the Book

The '60s saw an increase in broken homes. The Vietnam War was going on. There were three assassinations of prominent figures as well. In this tense political climate, Dr. Martin Luther King Jr. organized marches for higher or equal pay. Black folks without jobs were suffering from low income and wages, unlike their white counterparts. This meant that being adopted into a black home often was not about the welfare of the children; they adopted to supplement their income.

Many of the black homes were very abusive. I was puzzled about their idea of family, home, work, community, and how anyone would believe that they could achieve the "American Dream" by migrating here. Was their life that difficult in other places? I was sad to have to leave the Shaw home just because the social workers and society had a problem with a black kid in a white home. So, I returned to McClaren Hall and joined Tracy as we waited to be shipped out to the next foster home together. We were so young that I do not even know where she went while I was at the Shaw's or if she even went anywhere at all. Tracy just felt alright as long as she had me looking out for her.

Mr. and Mrs. Ross were the first black foster parents Tracy and I had together. They had three kids. I was young, so I can't recall their names. I do, however, remember that all of us received similar beatings. All the children slept in two rooms and shared big beds with a constant stench of urine. The bedding was rarely washed, and things were jam-packed all over the place. I remember them getting me two pairs of pants and two shirts, which I wore well into the next foster home. However, we were children, and we always played together. Interestingly, it turned out to be the black foster parents whom we needed protection from.

We were always hungry there. Mrs. Ross seemed to enjoy starving us whenever she was angry, be it about something she received in the mail, or a phone call, or one of the kids. Many times, if one kid did something wrong, then all the kids found out how to trim a rose bush switch. She mostly punished us with a switch, so that we would avoid trouble and stop others from putting us in trouble.

That changed eventually because I think she grew tired of beating four or five children consecutively. The school started questioning Tracy and me about the welts going up and down our legs. We didn't even have mealtime to look forward to because Mrs. Ross was also a horrific cook. She made macaroni and cheese with spoiled milk. This made me hate macaroni and cheese until I grew older. We always ate very little, and it tasted terrible. Even if the foster parents heard us say something about the bad-tasting food, they would make us eat it anyway. Mrs. Ross would usually warn me, "Sit there until you eat everything on your plate," and so I did. I spent several hours eating the horrible food and ended up going to bed sick and throwing it all up.

Sometimes the children, Tracy, and I went on quiet, nightly kitchen raids for food. We would crawl, tip-toe, whisper, and shush each other to steal some of the delicious left-overs from the kitchen. There were always plenty of little pecan pies in a private pantry drawer; tasty pecan pie was the item of choice. We were all in on these operations. Mrs. Ross sometimes left traps. She seemed to enjoy seeing us suffer. The food traps would allow her to see if something went missing at night. Sometimes she kept treats out that she knew we could not resist taking, like a cake with yellow frosting, in the refrigerator, not necessarily to make the heist more difficult, but to see what exact food we were stealing over-night.

We received a lot of whoopings at the Ross' foster home. When we were about to get a beating, Mrs. Ross would instruct us to go cut a switch from the rosebush in the backyard, and she trimmed off the thorns. The beatings got so bad that when she really wanted to hurt us, she left a few thorns on the switch. Tracy and I had welts and thorn holes on our legs from the constant beatings. One day, when I knew a beating was coming, I began to plot how to protect myself. I went to trim my rose bush switch, and I was instructed to leave some thorns in it. I was in trouble for stealing a pecan mini-pie from the refrigerator. I did it because I was starving. While I was making a switch from the backyard rosebush for my beating, I put a book in the back of my pants to protect myself from the pain. It did not work.

Mrs. Ross removed the book, and that was the worst beating ever. The social workers learned of this because it was not long after the school nurse discovered that Tracy and I had welts on our butts and legs. The social worker visited us at the Ross' home, and we told them. The social worker and Mrs. Ross traded dialog loudly, and when we showed them our legs, the social worker took us out of the Ross foster home. We stayed at McClaren Hall briefly and participated in several question-and-answer sessions with different psychological evaluators. Eventually we headed out to another foster home together. Our next foster parents were Mr. and Mrs. Jones.

Chapter 6

The Jones' Big Christmas

M r. and Mrs. Jones had two children named Michael and BB. This foster home started off well. They had a regular block of homes with craftsman appeal. The home had three bedrooms. BB and Tracy had a room. Michael and I had a room. Almost a normal setting of two parents. Mr. Jones worked as a garbage man. He was a happy guy I only saw briefly because he worked a lot. Mrs. Jones packed lunch, usually a peanut butter and jelly sandwich. I remember because I liked trading it with other students who had bologna sandwiches. We walked to school, lunch in-hand, across the train tracks near Slauson Boulevard and a junkyard.

Tracy and I were enrolled at 59th Street Elementary School. All of us in the Jones household walked to school every day. Michael Jones walked with his buddy. Tracy and BB walked together; they were of the same age. I walked with Stacy, my first-grade crush and bestie. I was in first grade, and Tracy was in kindergarten. I later learned through my brother, Steven's book, *The Hidden Dimension: An inside view on the reality of inner-city African America*, that Steven and Michael and Verna, were also at 59th Street for fifth and sixth grades, and that my big sister Gail was there for fourth grade.

Stacy was pretty with long, fluffy hair and pretty, red lips. Her lips stood out because of her light complexion. Having a beautiful best friend is not a bad way to start a new school in the first grade, one would think. Stacy lived with her grandma, who really liked me. They looked forward to me coming by and picking Stacy up on our way to school. She always yelled something out of the door, but I did not pay attention because I was just happy to see Stacy. Stacy had other problems, though, that I would encounter because of her beauty.

Bucky Heart, Bernard Beavers, and Donald Whitman also liked her. Before I came along, Bucky and Bernard always claimed that she was their girlfriend, but Stacy never agreed to that because she liked me. Back in those days, a girl might not have even known if a guy claimed her as his girlfriend. One day, Stacy and I were walking home from school. Across an open field junkyard by Slauson Avenue, across the railroad tracks, we ran into Bucky Heart, Bernard Beavers, and their crew. I became alert as they got closer. They wanted to fight me because Stacy and I were walking together, and they all knew she liked me. I said nothing; I did not have to. Stacy took charge. "If any of you lay a hand on him, you are going to have to answer to me," she stepped in between them and me, and there was no fight because she stood tough and pretty that day.

The teachers, social workers, and foster parents considered letting me skip a grade since I had a good command of the English language. After spending more time in school, I jumped from first to second grade, and this got me in over my head. Donald Whitman was in this class, and there was no more Stacy. The Whitman clan was huge. I believe they were 10 boys in the family, in different grades, throughout the elementary school. I was not afraid of Donald because he was shorter and smaller than me, but I was totally out of my league in that class. In the second grade, the girls acted quicker and more maturely when they liked you. Donald sat across from me and a girl who Donald claimed was his girlfriend. She would flirt with Donald but play with me under the desk. Sometimes she flashed me her anatomy, and me being the youngest in the class, did not know how to handle it, so I would raise my hand and report to the teacher. She denied it every time. It turned into a little game between us, but this pissed Donald off tremendously every day, so much that he wanted to beat me up or have his brothers beat me up for stealing his girlfriend.

One day it happened – an ambush. It was a regular lunch day, or so I thought. All ten of them were in the bathroom waiting for someone to lead me in. The Whitmans had more power. I was dragged into the toilet stall, and I recall the surrounding voices saying, "You better not hit him back," and other voices saying, "Hit him, Donald! Get him, Donald!" It seemed to go on for a long time, and no one broke it up. They had Donald beat me up as bad as little kids could beat someone up. To say the least, an ambush was just that – an ambush; you were still able to get up and walk away. It was more humiliating than painful. However, I took my beating and moved on with life. I started failing everything, and 59th Street School determined it was a mistake to skip me to a higher grade. I was sent back to my original grade, and BB, Tracy, and I were back in sync, one grade apart.

The Jones' foster home is where we were scared for lives. Tracy, Michael, BB, and I were molested by a visiting nephew of either Mr. or Mrs. Jones, who was given a babysitting job to watch us. He was not a professional babysitter. The Jones' had to go to work, so it was a convenience for him to watch us. He was visiting here from North Carolina, I believe. I was about 7 years old, Michael was 8, and BB and Tracy were 6. This traumatic experience occurred sometime before that Christmas. He was in his teens maybe 15, or 16. He starved us every day after the Jones went to work. To eat, we had to suck on his member. Every day, I would put up a fight or resist and sit for a long time. BB, Tracy, and Michael would be finished with their sucking, and they would be over their eating, and I would be sitting alone watching them eat. This nasty pervert with a big nappy afro would tell me that if I did it, then I could eat like them. I would sit with my arms folded, and my mouth poked out with fuming anger. But…I was starving. I just wanted to eat like the other children. So…I just closed my eyes and did it. The other kids would say, "Come on Darryl, you can do it, and then he will let you eat." I reluctantly crawled over there, looking at everyone. I was already on my knees. He put his thing in my mouth and told me to suck it. I really did not know what I was doing and wanted it to be over. I think he preferred the girls because they had to go longer. This went on for days. This horrible memory flashes in my dreams from time to time. The social workers and foster parents found out about this later. After days of intensive questioning, the boy was gone, leaving us all traumatized. Then, we had the biggest Christmas ever, with wall-to-wall toys to erase our memories.

Unfortunately, the molestations did not end there. Down at the corner house of the Jones' foster home lived a tall white man. Sometimes, when we were playing outside, the white man would come and watch us play hide and seek. There was a nice bush just made for hiding right alongside the Jones' house. This guy would make us hump each other in the bushes. He really got off on watching us hump in the bushes. Since I am a lover of history, I noticed that this happened around 1968 or 1969 when the porn movie industry was about to take off. I imagine people must have been very sexually repressed in those days. Anyway, the guy was undoubtedly a pedophile. BB and I were made to hump. Michael and Tracy were made to hump in the bush. Michael and BB were made to hump. When Tracy and I had to go into the bush, we would pretend we were humping to trick that dude. Tracy and I would sometimes get away with just rattling the bushes.

The way we got out of this foster home was strange. It was strange because it was the first time seeing our mother, Esther M. Lofton, in a long while. It was a normal day at 59th Street Elementary School at lunchtime. I was in the third grade then. I saw a black woman signaling me at the fence to walk over to her. The woman asked me if my name was Darryl. I was skeptical of her at first, for I had not seen my mother and father in four years. I was even more protective of her asking about Tracy. I was eight years old then, and Tracy was seven. I had only briefly known what our mother and father looked like, being only four when they were arrested, so when the strange woman asked, "Do I have a sister named Tracy?" I was confused why this woman was asking me about my sister and me. Slowly creeping out, she said that she was my mother. She looked kind of familiar, but honestly, I did not remember what my mother looked like. I think she said to not tell anyone she asked where Tracy was. I went and found Tracy.

A man and my mom were in the car; I called him Uncle Jim. He was not an uncle but a close friend of folks who helped our parents find and get us away from the first phase of being in the system. The next two years or so, we were united with our family, except Nina. Nina remained in foster care her entire life because she was placed in the system when she was just two months old, and she would have no memories of our parents. Sometimes, as time went by, we would be permitted to visit Nina to let her know of our existence. I really took this hard because all I wanted when I was little was to have my family back together. Nina had very religious foster parents, which is why she grasps religion more than my other siblings.

Tracy and I hopped into the car with our mom and Uncle Jim to head home for the first time in four years. From what I understand, my parents made a very good friend who was wealthy. Her name was Mrs. Edith Shaw. She owned apartments we were living in, while she was living in Florida. My parents managed the apartments unofficially in Inglewood. Mrs. Shaw did not like the ordeal my parents were going through, and she cared about us. We now had a little sister named Gena Ann Lofton. The years of spending time together as a family and getting to know each other were probably the greatest ever.

Chapter 7

First Time Reuniting with Family

Their new home was at 541 W. Manchester Blvd., Apt. #7, Inglewood CA. Tracy and I left home when we were three and four years old, respectively. We were now seven and eight years old, so I did not remember what anyone looked like. Standing in the parking lot when we pulled up was our father, Leon E. Lofton Jr., and our mother, Esther M. Lofton.

Mom pointed and said, "Darryl, that is your dad over there." I immediately sprinted towards him for I was so happy to be home. I jumped into my father's arms out of joy to know I still had a dad throughout this traumatic experience. (Running to jump in Father's arms would lose its magic after several returns as I grew older.) Tracy was also happy to be home. There was Michael, my oldest brother, stoic and stubborn, but who cared about everyone in the family. He wanted the family reunited and the lawsuit that my parents filed to be solved. But over the course of our lives, things didn't remain the same. The second oldest was Steven, and I remember him being almost the same as Michael, just huskier. They were big to me. They were never around when I needed brothers while getting my butt kicked but mentioning them sometimes curtailed an altercation or two. Then there was our oldest sister, Gail. Gail is my big sister who taught me never to hit girls. I thought that I could at least be number three in charge because I always believed that males were more dominant than females. Gail and I tested that by engaging in some small fisticuffs. Long story short, she beat me up, and my dad knocked me around a couple of times for hitting a girl. I learned to never hit girls. This altercation between Gail and me brought us even closer.

One day, I was at one of my forced tennis lessons at Inglewood High School. I say forced because I did not want to play, but my parents pushed me. I started showing up for the roll call, and then joining my buddies on the baseball diamond. We would also fool around in school because that's what mischievous kids did. I happened to see Gail pressed against the fence with this big gruesome Afro, wearing-a-leather-coat black guy – the type who probably would not pass muster at home with my folks. Gail and I made a deal that day that neither of us saw or knew anything about what the other was doing. Well now the secret is out! Don't really even think about it these days.

Tracy and I started to fight a lot due to our institutional competition for attention and dominance. The more institutionalized Tracy and I became, the farther we pushed away from each other's ideology. For the most part, I was more willing to buy into our parents' rules and laws, but Tracy resisted them because our parents had many old-fashioned ideas that she thought were too conservative, especially for the girls.

The beautiful part about these years was that it was the most family-oriented time in my life as a Lofton. We were poor in those apartments but wealthy in spirit like the Walton Family on

TV. We felt joy watching that show before bed, and we would act just like them and say "Goodnight, Michael! Goodnight, Steven! Goodnight, Gail! Goodnight, Darryl! Goodnight, Tracy! Goodnight, Gena!" Sometimes we would go overboard and keep going until we were told to be quiet.

As I said, we felt rich, even in that studio apartment. We had a new baby sister named Gena. The family ate meals together. We had homemade cornbread every night for dinner and ate meatloaf, spaghetti, chili, and liver and onions during the week. We had pancakes on Saturday mornings and biscuits on Sunday morning. Homemade and everything from scratch. The greatest fried chicken I ever had was my mother's and sister's back in those days. My piece was always the short thigh or the wing. Dad's piece was always one of the breasts.

Even though our parents were still not working, the house ran as if they were. Our parents were at war with the Los Angeles County School Board and every other bureaucracy that latched on to complicate our lives. The newspapers back then painted black parents like criminals, another form of a public lynching. The LA Sentinel, a black newspaper, eventually engaged my folks and were angry that my parents had not received any support from the black community. My dad would regularly say, "Son, if you take the government to court, a black man needs proper representation." They spoke of blacks being the only race in this country at that time without provincialism. Black folks were very upset with each other in the '60s, the same way blacks are angry with each other today in 2018. There are black people who are okay with being on welfare, while others just want opportunities to work. Lines can be drawn in the community because of this.

My parents were very organized and meticulous. Every week, there was a neighborhood paper that got swept up and thrown away. Dad would first have me go out on my bicycle and scoop up as many newspapers as possible. Then, he and our mom would sit up and cut out every coupon worth anything good and stack them up. A typical week of coupons would be: 20 Imperial margarine coupons for 1 pound for 10 cents with a $5 purchase; one dozen eggs for 10 cents with $5 purchase; a five-pound bag of sugar; 50 cents discount with $5 purchase. We would go to the supermarket with coupons and exact change in hand, and our mother would organize it all. I would have 10 cents, a coupon, and dozens of eggs in hand, for example. Then I would find a customer whose basket looked to be filled with a collection of items worth at least $5. To avoid becoming a nuisance to said customers, I would scan their cart, ensuring that the customer was not using the coupon themselves and did not have the items in the cart already. Then, I would say: "Excuse me Mr. or Mrs., I was wondering if I could give you the money and the coupon and the item to purchase for me since it looks like you will be making a five-dollar purchase."

It worked most times because we were not stealing or begging, and people respected the fact that our parents had the dignity to handle the circumstances at hand and their disenfranchisement without disturbing the lives of others. The kitchen, pantry, and freezer had an organization. Twenty bags of flour, ten bags of sugar, baking soda, ten boxes of cornmeal; you name it, it was stocked. We always had all the necessary staples because Mom made everything from scratch. The freezer and refrigerator had several pounds of butter and a half gallon of milk. All coupon items. Dad loved dessert, so it came after every dinner, which was served every day at 5:00pm. You better be on time! The supplies did not happen overnight. These were weekly chores. It became an urban hunting and gathering process.

We also did daily chores, cleaning, mending, sweeping, and swabbing. Men did men work, and women did women work. Oh, how I wanted to learn to cook. I would hang in there for hours talking to mom observing how she unraveled the kitchen and organized it. I was allowed to sit there and taste test. I loved raw cake batter and licking the icing knife. She would call one of the girls to do kitchen work, like make some corn-bread. Cornbread was made every day because it was cheap, lasted a long time, and could feed our large family. The girls learned most of the cooking. Now I did have a job. A boy job was usually outside, taking out the trash, cleaning the kitchen, which entailed clearing and washing all the cabinets. Those days, we had no mops. I cleaned the floors on all fours with a scrub-brush and tried to reach all corners. Every week, the boys rotated this duty. Cleaning the kitchen was a hard, ardu-ous duty, but I appreciated the lesson.

What became the most difficult to tolerate was the change in personality. It would often feel like our parents were using us, children, to make their statement. There were regular lectures about things they read in the newspaper that angered them. One time, our parents sent us to school barefoot to say, "If a parent is denied the right to work, then how can they properly clothe and feed their children?" Many of the lectures were over my head and didn't fully make sense to me. Our parents sometimes kept us from going to school to cause a state of "moral panic" and somehow raise attention and awareness of their cause – The Loftons vs. the Los Angeles County School Board. But I always wondered, if you do not send me to school to receive an education, then how can I understand what you are trying to teach me?

Chapter 8

Hannibal Hayes and Kid Curry

I met another best friend while living at 541W. Manchester Blvd. #7. His name was Dennis Krotzer, and he had a brother named Keith Krotzer, three sisters named Tyan, Lianne, and Laura, and a wiener dog named Heidi. Dennis was a good friend to have during this early part of life. Looking back, our whole block was comprised of different ethnic minorities.

A friend and classmate of ours was Joyce Lee. She was brilliant and kind. Her parents, who owned a 4-unit apartment complex, wanted her to succeed, and so they made her study every day. Her parents did not want her out ripping and racing around the neighborhood. I genuinely felt that the world we live in was just divided by black and white, where everyone that was not black or mixed with black was white. However, here Joyce Lee and her family were doing great. Honestly, while growing up, no one ever sat down and explained to me that many different cultures exist in an American neighborhood.

Mr. Krotzer was a decorated Korean War veteran of German-American ethnicity, and Mrs. Krotzer was Korean-American. They were a part of an influx of Korean War veterans in the community, and my dad was a WWII veteran. I understood later in life why they never became friends. They, however, respected each other. Once, my father explained his case against the Los Angeles School Board, and their relationship took a more serious tone. Dad was always good at explaining what he believed in. Although if or when my dad had issues with the law, Mr. Krotzer knew they gave black men a hard time.

I spent a lot of time playing with Dennis and Keith. Dennis had a brand-new, shiny, blue stingray bicycle with the fancy new banana seats. My dad had just built me a Green Huffy stingray with knock-off spare parts from broken-down bicycles. All of our bikes in the family were either built by my dad, Mike, Steve, or me. My dad made sure I knew everything there was about bicycles. I cleaned down to the bearings of each wheel shaft to the interiors of the pedal casing. I was out riding when I met Dennis. Those early days, we shared the life of things seen on TV. For example, we saw a race between two famous drag racers: The Green Monster vs. The Blue Flame. My green make-shift Huffy was the Green Monster, and Dennis had the Blue Schwinn Stingray called the Blue Flame.

Sometimes, I won and other times he did. Another program we watched on television was *Alias Smith & Jones*, which was about two outlaws and a gang. It featured Hannibal Hayes, alias "Mr. Smith," played by Pete Dual and Kid Curry, alias "Mr. Jones," played by Ben Murphy. (When Pete died, we gave a newspaper clipping funeral. Sad day. RIP.) Everyone who had a bicycle in the neighborhood road with us. This was during the time period from 1968 – 1970 when Inglewood was expanding and underdeveloped. They were expanding City Hall, and there were giant holes and

My Dad, Leon E. Lofton Jr.

lots of dirt on which to ride bikes. Whenever we found dirt hill developments, we were jumping dirt bikes.

Dennis was a great repairman, too. He really loved tinkering with engines with his dad. In class, he always drew sketches of cars. He grew up to be the mechanic and owned his shop. I thought I would become a race car driver, but life had other plans. Between the 4th grade when we met and my back-and-forth between institutions and home, Dennis, Keith, and I kept in touch before I left for the Navy. At least the stability of our friendship was something I could count on.

Chapter 9

The Bussing Experience was Unequal and Separate

Tracy and I lived with our family. Dennis and Keith and their family were my neighborhood friends. It was around 1970, and we all were getting bussed out to Warren Lane Elementary School. The purpose was to get some of us minorities integrated into the white classes. The first day the bus arrived at the new school, all the black students got off. We walked across the playground to the bungalows that were put there for our classrooms. Dennis and Keith went to the classes to mix in with the white students. We were all minorities, it's just that the black minority was different. Integration was not going to work for us. Brown vs. Board of Education was not doing the work that it was supposed to do. It was to end separate but equal (segregation) and old Jim Crow. Here it was in 1970, 16 years after the court ruling, getting bussed into a segregated situation. I believed all the battles related to segregation at this time should be used to advance my parents' case, but they kept insisting that their situation was not about race or discrimination. It was about the black code of the law. Black code of law is when the laws on the books carry a different meaning, when they pertain only to black people.

The court system and the NAACP wanted to try every black grievance case as test cases. Our family was already broken apart and distributed into the system, with lives shattered. Our parents were not handled with due process or equal protection of law at this point, and they felt that they were not treated as American citizens. We must really understand the silent era and the civil rights era. People were angry but they were afraid of Jim Crow laws. While the civil rights period brought on public outrage and anger, my parents still expressed most of their rage in private. They were still protesting freely, loudly, and publicly, but at home I would overhear them having heated discussions about what they were facing out in the world. Their anger would sometimes result in lectures to us. But anger eventually moves fear to the side. It was a very volatile time.

My dad and I would go for long walks at night. It was his way of getting exercise. He was the main one restricted to the house. I did not understand why things were that way. I had to grow up and read our history. I had to realize what my parents were up against. I am 57 years old now and better educated, and I put myself into the thought process of my father during our walks and our conversations of past. We walked late at night because of safety and privacy. My father truly believed that he could not walk alone anywhere. If he was ever alone walking day or night, he felt quite unsafe because the police might stop him and pin him with charges. The law was unjust.

Bussing was a joke. Brown vs. Board of Education was the greatest trick ever played on the black community. It took away

black empowerment and took away jobs from the black community. Each state used the ruling of Brown vs. Board of Education
to advance their own agenda. My parents' anger with politicians
was that the black ones allowed this to happen. I am older now,
and I read stories and periodicals of how none of the clerks on the
Supreme Court wanted to work for Thurgood Marshall and that
the clerks were the ones really doing all of the work. I witnessed
that bussing was a joke. I even realized that integration was a ruse.

I headed over to the bungalows every school day because I
was black. In the bungalows, we tore paper in half, broke pencils
in half, and sharpened them to have enough supplies for everyone
to have something to write on and with. In the white classrooms,
Dennis and Keith received books, paper, and pencils. They were a
different type of minority. They were mixed Korean and German.
In those days, if your father was white, you were white. If there was
any trace of black in you, then you were black. That was due to the
ruling of Plessy vs. Ferguson in 1896. Plessy looked white but had
a percentage of black in him, so he was made to sit at the back of
the train. This case made Jim Crow legal. It established Separate
but Equal. It made drinking out of same drinking fountain a crime.
It made using the same bathrooms a crime. It made stepping off
or aside on the sidewalk when passing a white person law. Not
until 1954 with the ruling of Brown vs. Board of Education was
separate supposedly not equal. But I still experienced inequality in
the bungalows in 1970 during my bussing experience. My parents
were disillusioned. Although this integration experience was devastating, life moved forward, and we advanced.

In the 5th grade, we had the most memorable talent show. I
was not in it, but I was genuinely entertained by it. We all had

something to be proud of. In the talent show, there were two main events. In 1970, the two best singing groups at the time were the Jackson 5 and Donny Osmond and the Osmond Brothers. The two most popular songs out were *One Bad Apple* by the Osmonds and *ABC* by the Jackson 5, and both were performed at the talent show. That night gave both black children and white children something to be proud of. It was the first time I witnessed a crossover of black and white culture. That day, white people liked black music, and black people liked white music. I loved both songs and sang to them whenever I heard them on the radio.

Another experience in the 5th grade was when our parents decided to send us to school barefooted. This was a form of protest and to make a statement to the Los Angeles School Board. My parents thought it was a good time to show the School Board that parents cannot clothe, feed, and put shoes on the feet of their children without gainful employment. Remember my parents wanted to stay as far away from racial discrimination as they could, which I felt was the fear they carried from the silent era and mystified clampdown effect of Jim Crow. Not long after that, we were on our way back to McClaren Hall because after the barefoot stunt, our parents were notified that being barefooted was not allowed. My parents' next stunt was to not send us to school. Our parents were again arrested and off to McClaren Hall we went.

Before I returned to McClaren Hall, a few other things were happening in Inglewood. Our parents were not really religious. I would equate it more to hanging onto fears and superstitions, mainly since our dad was the son of a Methodist minister. Our grandparents were Methodist, and our dad was the preacher's son and the "bad kid." We attended some Methodist services so that we were introduced to religion, but we had a choice whether to go or not. What we received from the church was a YMCA membership to learn to exercise and have recreation. I learned how to steam and sauna as a child and I still indulge today.

Our parents also made sure we played board games, cards, and with dolls, cars and trucks. Often our parents would play with us. A big match our dad joined in on was Monopoly. I held my own, but I beat my little sister Gena a lot at Monopoly; I bought everything, which doubled my chances and gave the best edge. Well, I hear little Gena is a big-time Realtor between California and New York nowadays. My dad taught me to play chess at around the 4th grade. We spent time matching wits on the chess board. I was not sure at first if he was kidding me and allowing me to beat him or not. He taught me to keep my composure whether I won or lost. While being held out of school, our indoor entertainment also consisted of reading and mathematics. My experience with my dad's teaching was that it turned physical. I had the hardest time with fractions. Adding and subtracting mixed fractions was my "Achilles heel." Occasionally, out of frustration, my dad would bop me upside the back of the head when I gave an incorrect answer. As I aged, it became apparent that hitting meant teaching to him. It made me flinch when someone stood over me.

I developed a love for cutout paper dolls. I played a lot with Tracy and Gena. I thought I was the ultimate fashion designer, and my dad hated every minute of it. He would say, "If you played chess more, this game would help you analyze things in real life." My dad saw that I was gaining interest in cooking and designing clothes, and he felt that he needed to put an abrupt end to that. "My son will not play with dolls," he would say. I liked designing clothes. I began playing with them in McClaren Hall when I was introduced to my first book of cut-out dolls. I became so proficient that I could make my own drawings, outfits, and color schemes. Dad ended it. I got in trouble for getting corn-rows put in my hair, and I was not even living with him. I was living in a foster home at the time but my parents would look for us and find us. Dad would show up at the foster home to chastise me, saying there would be no corn rows and no earrings. I had to take them all out. He was still controlling my life.

Looking back, I now understand. My parents were in a battle with the state of California. They wanted to maintain parental control of their soldiers. My dad was trained in guerrilla warfare; he was the last of the Buffalo Soldiers. We children had to start addressing him by "Yes Sir" and "No Sir." I could have easily started gang-banging out there on my own, in the foster homes, or in the boys' homes. But my dad would fight me tooth and nail before he ever gave into gang-banging, and I think his surprise visits were what got both sides playing hide-the-children. The social workers and the foster parents did not like those unexpected visits. They were also beginning to upset us and become more controlling. Mind control would be all that our parents had left to maintain control of our decisions when we were taken away. The old game of catch-and-release, as played during slavery days, seemed to be taking hold in my life. I was feeling like I had been in and out of McClaren Hall and the foster homes so many times, that I was being returned home just to be removed again. It was about this time that I came to understand that my parents would do something to provoke a response by their opponent, whether it was the Board of Education, the School District, or their own children. From here I will describe the first break away from 541 W. Manchester Blvd. #7, when my parents went defiant against DSS, somewhere around 5th grade.

Chapter 10

Religious Whack-a-Mole

When the actions of my parents again resulted in our being taken out of our home, Gena was still too young to go, I was 9, and Tracy was 8. Nina was still in the foster home she had been since she was two months old. Mike, Steve, and Gail were approaching the age they would be released from such care, and Tracy and I were approaching the junior high level. The institutional lifestyle lent more stability and comfort, at least for Tracy and me.

We were introduced to dating and dances. The facility was under construction, and for the life of me, I never understood why some kids wanted to escape. I would also hear rumors that my big brothers, Michael and Steve (nicknamed Sugar Bear, like the cereal), had escaped, making me popular and protected on the junior block (in my mind, anyway). In the morning, getting dressed was easy at first, but then I realized that girls would be in classes with us. I started seeing the slow transition of grooming myself. Kids would be released, and others would check in. I felt myself becoming cocky and mouthy. I began playing chess with my 5th- 6th-grade teacher and beating him. He was just like my dad, waiting for the next chance to beat me. The combination of playing chess and the power to control my situation became apparent. I was learning the system and how to get favors inside the institution. Extra food, new issue clothes, comfortable cleaning assignments, and messenger duty. I had fun socializing with the female assigned to messenger service. Sometimes on school days, students were assigned messenger duty, a boy and a girl, to relay information back and forth between the main offices, the school building, and the wings where we lived. Sometimes, in passing on a message, one could fool around in the bushes or find a private nook to make out with a girl.

In the 5th grade, Tracy and I were sent to another foster home. The older kids – Mike, Steve, and Gail – were shipped off to their own foster homes. I also heard that Michael was able to return with our parents because he was an adult at age 18. Tracy and I were sent to the Pennington's home, which had profound meaning in my life.

During this time, I was introduced to Methodism by my parents but wasn't forced to partake in it. The Ross' were Baptist. I remember seeing that word on some of the churches they frequented. Yes, they traveled around to churches with long names, such as The Holy Trinity, or The Divine Church of Jesus Christ.

The Jones family adhered to a belief in the Holy Trinity, and the church would gather us in the center of the sanctuary where all the children had to wash away what we had previously been taught. I grew up being told that Jesus was the son of God. The followers of this church taught us that Jesus was God. The adults physically forced us to chant, "Thank you, Jesus," and I often felt them squeeze my shoulder and speak with anger under their breath when I chose not to conform or grew tired of chanting.

At McClaren Hall, I attended Catholic and Methodist services, and they all had their ways of communion. I enjoyed the tiny taste of crackers and grape juice shots. Attending church services was voluntary. I usually attended when I wanted to get out of doing something, or I wanted to meet up with a girl. The Penningtons, however, were Seventh-Day Adventists. The Pennington's were interesting. The religion promotes good health and about 50% of the church members are vegetarian. We went to church on Saturdays and every Friday, we had to fast for the entire day. I hated starving myself. We were doing and living everything Seventh-Day Adventist. It did not stick, though. Religion felt more burdensome than anything, but I continued to harbor superstitions and a fear of the unknown until I began to read and learn about history and philosophy later in life.

Another observation was that they already had three kids that were about the same ages we were, and then one who was a few years older. We were there to supplement their income. The home was in Carson, California. The area in which our neighborhood was located was called Centerview, and Compton was across the train tracks. This was important to know because Centerview was "Pyrue" territory and in Compton was for the "Crips."

Tracy and I were enrolled at Ardmore Elementary School for 4th and 5th grade respectively. Here, I was coaxed into my first black-on-black fight in a Compton neighborhood where our church was located. (My first black vs. white fight was for respect and acceptance of getting bussed.) In Centerview, the area had more upscale, black-owned homes, and the neighborhood was just beginning to show signs of graffiti-sprayed painting on walls, indications of the growth of gang life. I noticed a Centerview gang called The Pyrues, and I would see graffiti taking up residence on buildings. I also heard rumors of all the gang activity across the railroad tracks, but it did not bother us because we were usually inside for the evenings.

Compton was a blue collar area and the territory of opposing gangs. Again, this was just the chatter of little kids who did not have any direct contact with gangs. Another pastime for Tracy and me was helping the church with custodial duties, which was Mr. Pennington's side job. While cleaning the church one Thursday evening, I had my first encounter with some of the kids in Compton. They came around starting trouble and showed off in front of all of us, acting real tough. I was 10, and I remember being scared inside but maintained a poker face. The gang leader bumped my chest with his chest as if to coerce me to throw the first punch. My knowledge of the stability of the game of chess helped me to calculate my actions. For several seconds, the two of us circled each other, and we continued to bump each other's chest. Gazing out of the peripherals of my eyes, I could see Mr. Pennington smirking with joy. I was silently angry because I wished he would have stepped in to break it up before we started wrestling on the floor. This went on for several minutes, and I could see Mr. Pennington enjoying every moment of it because he felt he had someone who could have his back, or at least provide some interference for him in that terrain filled with violent youth. His two sons were standing on the side, completely alarmed and shocked along with everyone else. At times, the oldest son would make me feel like I was even superior to him. I rolled with it. I was able to bump chests with these dudes because I had done this same dance in McClaren Hall. I received nothing but praise for not cowering to those thugs even though I was scared to death.

At the Pennington foster home, I had a near-death experience. Soon after that, the Pennington's relinquished the foster care program. We were all out on our bikes one afternoon, and I was standing straddling a bicycle with a leg on each side. The front and side lawns were sloped on our corner lot. While standing there, I slowly watched a vehicle veer out of control and drive up onto the sidewalk, coming directly at me. I had no time to scream or panic. Chess strategizing immediately came into survival calculations. *How do I move? What should I do?* I allowed the vehicle to hit my bike first as my leg moved to the protected side. As if in slow motion, my left leg slowly inched back to join the back side of my right leg. I found myself in the crack of the slope of grass and the pavement, which spared my life. I was still squirming as the car came up on the sidewalk, crushing my bike. The result was the car and driver on top of a bicycle which was on top of me. A couple of kids ran to get an adult. I squirmed my way out and went to look for help. I immediately saw a firetruck approach. I stopped and stared as Mrs. Pennington came over to talk to me. The firemen started doing medical tests on me, and I checked out alright. By the time it was all over, the driver of the vehicle was talking to police while the police made this guy touch his nose with a finger. He was explaining to the police his version of what had happened as we headed into the house for veggie burgers. Little did I know that this event would be just one of many where I felt I'd been wrongly run over.

Chapter 11

Hide-the-Salami

Following this episode, Tracy and I found ourselves heading to a new foster home, a result of what I refer to as a game of hide-the-salami. My foster parents would inform the Department of Social Services that they spotted our parents driving around the neighborhood, or the school would make a report to the foster parents of a sighting, who would, in turn, report the information to the social workers. We were shipped off to another foster home or back for a short stay at McClaren Hall whenever this happened. This time, we did not go back to McClaren Hall. We went directly to another foster home in Pomona, California: the Mr. and Mrs. Price foster home.

By that time, our parents were getting really close to regaining custody of us. Something was worked out with the courts to allow them to do so, but it was a brief stay. So there we were in the Price household where I was introduced to real humping and grinding naked. The Price home had an older son of about 17 years old who was rarely present. They had an older foster girl who was fourteen. I was 11 then. She would sneak into my bed. She just wanted me to get on top of her and hump. I don't even remember her name.

The Price's had another little foster daughter named Jeanine, who was Tracy's age and about to turn my age. One afternoon, we were all out in a yard celebrating Jeanine's eleventh birthday. Jeanine was very flirty. She was very fast for her age. At times, when we were running around playing she would grab my torso and pull my hips into her front as if to hint at humping. The next thing that happened was the older foster brother crashed the party with a couple of his buddies. He grabbed Jeanine's arm and pulled her into an area in the backyard with a swinging gate. Five minutes later, he exited, zipping up his pants. I looked in on Jeanine, and she was crying and lying on the ground with soiled panties and her dress up. I was witnessing the ugly aftermath of an innocent child whose virginity was taken by an older relative of the family tasked with protecting us. This was at the house of the Price family. Shortly after this incident we were released and sent home to 541 W. Manchester Blvd. #7.

Home again, Tracy was 10, and I was 11. I was about to complete 6th grade at Warren Lane Elementary School, along with the attempt at school desegregation and the bungalows, half sheets of paper, broken pencils and all black students. I was off to Crozier Jr. High for the 7th grade. I vividly remember age eleven because I experienced real jail time. I was caught stealing and was scared straight. We had a childhood YMCA membership sponsored by the Methodist church program. I loved Hot Wheels, and I had to have them. I became fascinated with Hot Wheels because we never really received many toys when we returned to live with our parents. So, occasionally while out riding bikes with Dennis and Keith, my Inglewood buddies did a lot of dumpster diving. Another one of my assignments while out riding and playing with my friends was to always be on the lookout for bottles. Recycling bottles and newspaper collecting contributed to the family grocery bill. While dumpster diving, I found Hot Wheels and track pieces, along with toys, games, Playboy magazines to make our clubhouse (an abandoned garage) a fun place to hang out. My mother and father began to inquire about where I was getting all those Hot Wheels. I replied, "I just find them."

A YMCA buddy, who also had a massive Hot Wheels collection, joined in on my capers. I was a habitual thief. I began hitting department stores for Hot Wheels. I was in Sears one afternoon, instead of working out at the gym. They had a beautiful collection of Hot Wheels. I fingered and gazed at almost every one of them, but I decided to go down to Grants Department store first. I began lifting (stealing) Hot Wheels. I kept telling my parents that I found all my new Hot Wheels in trash cans and they bought it hook, line, and sinker – mainly because Dad was so happy about the money I brought home by collecting and returning bottles and cans that allowed us to go to Millers Market to pick up some bread, milk, flour or cornmeal.

My amateur thievery was so successful that I had another friend at the YMCA who also liked Hot Wheels and wanted to come along. Lesson one, do not commit crimes; if you do, always work alone. The two of us were at a Sear's department store, and immediately when they saw the two of us, a silent alarm went off. I saw one, two, three people in different areas appearing to shop slowly circling. Then, my buddy was oblivious to the door, and at that moment I already had my car down my pants. The employees were hawking us hard. Deep down, I wanted my buddy's first time to be successful. I did not get to get busted with him. By this time, I was still quite the rookie. They were onto us, and I did not want to surrender. I could have made the decision to put the car back and have my buddy do the same. No one would have been in trouble. I did not. We thought we were leaving the store like shoppers who had decided not to make a purchase, but plain clothes detectives were circling the building. I learned that day how security teams work. Off to jail we went.

I was scared to death. My greatest worry was what my dad was going to do to me. I wanted to go home, but also didn't. I'd committed a petty crime. I arrived at the jail with my friend around 3 p.m. We were both eleven years old. The next ten or so hours could have been a script prepared for that '80s show, *Scared Straight*. We were crying, and my friend was blaming it all on me. At 6 p.m. my friend's parents had come to pick him up. We had already been interrogated for an extended period and lectured on how crime did not pay. My cell had an unstable character in there talking trash to the officers. He was a grown-up black man. While in the cell he made me feel at ease. At the same time, I was utterly scared of him. He also talked to me about what's to come when confronted by my parents. None of what he said happened, but it helped to calm me.

For the first phase of suspense, my parents let me sit in jail until close to midnight before coming to get me. Charges were dropped because we were kids. I got home, ate, bathed, and went to bed. Still, Dad and Mom were pissed. The next morning came a lecture about how my actions jeopardized the family pursuit for due process and equal protection under the law since I should be conducting myself as a law-abiding citizen. A black man hinders the struggle for equality when he commits a crime and becomes the criminal. After that morning lecture (one of several lectures to come), we children got dressed and headed out for school. "Wait, Darryl," my dad said as he grabbed my shoulder. "You wait here." My brothers and sisters looked at me with shock. We all knew that I may not be alive when they returned home from school that day. This is a taste of the fear that I would forever feel from my father. This beating for stealing was with his fist and feet. Another was with a belt after receiving a swat from the principal back in the 5th grade for leaving school campus at lunchtime. That must have been before going barefoot to school. After that beating, he was the meanest person to me. On top of that, nothing in the life with our family would happen with ease. From that day on, the only focus for each of my parents was winning case #895188. It became an obsession, and all of us children became the tools used by those on both sides of the battle.

Chapter 12

The Department of Social Services (DSS) Wages War on the Loftons

The Lofton family had day-to-day lectures about conduct, almost like a sergeant would give a morning brief to his platoon. I realize now that's where Dad got that from because I had another windbag a time or two while in the Navy. He would tell us to, first, always be observant of strange vehicles approaching and people walking up towards apartments. I blew this assignment right off the track. I learned my parents were at war the hard way. I was handed a subpoena one day from someone in a vehicle who had handed it to me. The guy on the passenger side rolled down his window and said, "Hey kid! Take this into the house to your parents." I said "OK." For a moment I thought I was doing something official and honorable. Once I handed it to my dad, the vehicle sped off after ensuring that my father received it. Out of the corner of my eye, I could see the guy making sure that I handed the envelope to my dad.

I could see and feel the anger and disgust burning inside my father, at them and at me. At that moment, I realized that the DSS was battling against my dad. I began to see how we were treated nicely and then dumped somewhere new, just to destroy my family. They were like an opponent in a game of chess. I knew at that moment that I needed to be a better soldier for the front line of bureaucratic warfare.

Brown vs the Board of Education also divided blacks who were fortunate enough to find teaching jobs and black political activists, and this was evident in the way those teachers treated the children of those activists. I experienced being singled out and one incident stands out in my mind even today. I was in the 7th grade at Cozier Jr. High School and was humiliated by a black male teacher who singled me out of a group who continued playing after being told to stop. He said, "I listened to my parents and did what they told me to do." He said more than that in an attempt to put me in my place and insisted I deliver the message to my father.

I probably should have, but by this time, my mental defense mechanism had been wired to handle my own battles. It was not as though I wasn't facing similar struggles about dignity and respect with my own father. This battle was really beginning to form in my mind and all around. We would have to watch the news every day to stay informed. I was always forced to watch the news, but it was now that I really started paying attention. Guys on the news were getting beatdowns for their leather jackets and tennis shoes. Memories of watching the news with my parents go way back to when President Kennedy was shot. I recall the coverage of that and remember watching little John-John Kennedy waving at the crowd.

I looked forward to the commercials because they were more entertaining than the news, but I slowly began enjoying watching the news coverage. Race was always the underlying issue even though my parents insisted on avoiding the subject. This issue was purely economical because many of the bad actors were blacks inflicting these attacks on my parents. The decision in Brown v. Board of Education was the reason my parents were not teachers anymore. The issue pitted black against black. The reason they left Baltimore in the first place was to find teaching jobs, but opportunities for black professionals involved strange politics in most parts of the country and my parents became angry over their plight. Both of them even ran for office later in this ordeal. There were times when my parents felt that if they ran for office, they could get the story out. Then, DSS would begin hiding the children, which explains all the foster homes and institutions. Tracy and I would go through two to three more foster homes together, and they would eventually swallow up Gena and a new baby sister named Heather Leigh Lofton, too. Hubert Heffner was my little joking nickname I gave to my baby sister. Eventually, the DSS could not place Tracy or me in any more foster homes, so they started sending Tracy to girl's institutions and me to boy's institutions.

After a couple of years, my parents promised the courts that they would become good actors, so Gena and Heather only did a couple of years in foster care. Only once did our parents prove to the courts that they could provide a home for them. Older siblings began working, and they purchased a home. Back to Inglewood for the last stay at 541 W. Manchester Blvd.

Chapter 13

The Teenage Experience

This time back in Inglewood, I attempted the old ritual of jumping in my father's arms, but it did not feel right, because I was not happy to see him. I was bigger and older. By that time, we children were getting exhausted by the whole ordeal. Even Michael hated it, and he was the eldest. If only he could have mustered up the courage to admit it. I had witnessed that guy taking many smacks across the face, and it happened more frequently as we grew older. It made me afraid of having any exchanges with our father. All the other kids felt the same way, except for Gena. She was too young to be the target of our parents' rage in its fullest sense. That could be why she was so successful in life; our parents' dominance did not destroy her spirit. When Gena and Heather returned home, our parents wanted to do things right this time for the children's education. The two of them were enrolled in a Catholic School. They both received better training than the rest of us and with fewer interruptions. She and Heather came along after our parents promised the courts that the shenanigans would stop.

While Gena and Heather were not afraid to respond to our parents like the rest of us were, Heather did express how she was having difficulty dealing with the overbearing nature our parents had. I assumed their dominance may have been harder on her because she was the only one there and still at a young age. Dad loved to single us out, at least giving the rest of us some bit of a reprieve if only for a short while. I remember one time our brother Steve didn't respond to dad's badgering in a manner my father thought acceptable, which only led to him becoming more hostile. Dad got right in Steven's face. He liked to get real close to ensure he was the only one speaking. It would happen so fast, and all you could see was someone holding the side of your face. Then he would assume a challenging stance, saying, "Come on, hit me." When his challenge wasn't accepted he would begin whaling away on his target with punches.

Steven took a beating for a disagreement in our parent's constant black-bashing. Now, he is one of the biggest Trump supporters. Go figure. When my father could no longer target Steven because he left home to join the Navy, my parents painted him as a villain who had abandoned his family during our time of need.

We occupied three apartment storage units, and the sleeping quarters were separated by gender. The folks would continue to stay in the main unit #7. The boys stayed in #6, and the girls were down in #3. We got to know our Jewish neighbor pretty well. His name was Jodie Beanstalk, a quiet, bald hippie out of the late '60s generation. He smoked pot, drove a VW bug, and was a mild hipster and cool dude. He lived in #8. One time, his place was raided by mistake and turned upside down because the police said they really wanted our dad's place. They were lying. That was just how business was done when police wanted to invade your privacy illegally, according to Mister Beanstalk.

He wasn't the only one having to deal with the police. My parents had a number of issues of their own, as they always did. This time around, my brother Steve and my Dad had a fight because Steve was tired of the drama that caused so much instability for us kids. My parents actions resulted in a 30-day stint in jail, leaving my brother Mike in charge. Talk about a 30-day festive party in Inglewood. We played outside some days until 11pm, and we really got to see what the other kids, who had a more relaxed household, did outside. Without a curfew we played with friends until they had to go inside, as long as it did not get back to our parents. Those were the most exciting days ever in my childhood life with our parents, but it was a result of their being in jail, with the older kids left in charge. We usually had to be home by 5pm every day for dinner. Not while our parents were in prison though. No school, no curfew, no rules, and no parents. Then it came to an end. Not long after this, we were on our way to our last trip to McClaren Hall together. The day before, I had entered ninth grade at Inglewood High School. I had only seen Dennis a few more times after this because our schedules were different, so my day was filled with loneliness rather than fun. With the reputation of my family's jail time and other trouble with the school and the police, I had few friends. Add to this an issue of distrust and paranoia on the part of my parents, particularly living in the black community, and it was a sheltered and lonely childhood.

One black family did move onto the block, and I enjoyed playing with their kids. Their names were Skip, Sporty, and an older brother named Michael, and they were all cool with me. We got along well. Our parents would give lectures explaining why they were on welfare and how the system was set up to guide black people to collect welfare instead of gainful employment. Our parents felt that other blacks were giving in too quickly to welfare instead of joining the fight with them. It was at this point I began to relate our parents' ordeal to the Milagros bean field wars in Mexico.

Steve was in the Navy, and Mike and Verna were their teens now. They did not have to return home. 541 W. Manchester was destroyed entirely during a raid. It seemed like the City of Inglewood and the powers that be, were intent on destroying my family, and the black politicians turned a blind eye, stood by, and allowed it to take place. That would be the theme of all my father's lectures. He and my mother had never been convicted of a crime, but everything that was happening to my family was in retaliation for them filing case number #895188 in the Superior Court of Los Angeles: Leon and Esther Lofton vs. The Los Angeles County School Board.

Chapter 14

Back to McClaren Hall: Teens

The *L.A. Times* documents a bed shortage at McClaren Hall in a March 24, 1966 article:

> Mac Hall was run like a jail, with "perimeter security measures, which include floodlights and a 14 feet chain link fence, topped by five feet of wire mesh (barbed wire)," according to a 1960 *L.A. Times* article. (Charles Gould, *Los Angeles Times*, New MacLaren Hall to House Juvenile Wards: Sister Kenny Polio Hospital Being Converted by Probation Department, (1960, November 6), p. sg1.) It turns out that the Probation Dept. ran Mac Hall throughout the 40s – 70s, and thus, it was run the way they ran their prisons. They even hired "women probation attendants" via an ad run in the *L.A. Times* in 1961. *(Los Angeles Times*, Workers Sought for Hall Jobs, (1961, January 15), p. sg_a15.) Eventually, County Social and Health Services ran Mac Hall. (Kirsten Anderberg, Ventura, CA.)

The above quote is from an author who gave a different description of the facility. I do remember that it was a very hard place for white kids. The author also describes it as a place where children get punished for their parents' crimes. Different ethnicities were trying to escape. That explains my institutionalization. Tracy and I liked it there. We eventually wanted the place to become home, which was not going to happen. At 15 years old, I had asked a social worker if I could just stay at McClaren Hall until I reached 18.

This time Tracy, Heather, Gena, and I were there. Heather was new to all of it, although she did spend some time, I believe, in a foster home with Tracy and Gena. I recall visiting them at that time. They really tried to keep us together in pairs this time. McClaren Hall had been remodeled and was really nice. By now we had been back and forth so many times that the place felt like a home to us, and we loved it. I was now respected as one of the big kids with a widespread reputation for being there so many times. Tracy and I pretty much felt that McClaren Hall was our home. We grew up there. When we thought we were there too long, we would pray that they would not call us up for release. The dances were fun. The girls were pretty, and I had a kind of gangster reputation without becoming a gangster.

This time, I met and dated many girls. Some were brief because of the way people came and left McClaren Hall. Some relationships continued for short stints outside McClaren Hall. I dated a Yolanda, and we visited each other once, then it never happened again. I dated a Christine, and we had a couple of brief phone calls, and that fizzled. But Star… Her name was really Estrella Mayo at the time. We dated outside while I was sent to California

Youth homes. It was also brief. In fact, she took up with another guy in the boys' home. We ran into each other again, and I will explain our brief encounters later when I was in my last boys' home and after my first weekend in the US Navy boot camp.

Tracy and I were placed together in a foster home and Gena and Heather in another. By this time, the courts and the social workers had already started a battle with my parents. The Los Angeles foster homes were exhausted and shifted us out to Pomona for foster home jumping. The beginning of my educational shakeup had already begun; we were moved around from foster home to foster home and back and forth with our parents so many times that we had attended Warren Lane Elementary, Oak Street Elementary, 59th Street Elementary School, Center-view Elementary school, McClaren Hall Elementary, Crozier Jr. High, Horace Mann Jr. High, Norco Jr. High, McClaren Hall Jr. High, California Youth Home High, Inglewood High, Ganesha High, McClaren Hall High, Juvenile Hall High, and Los Angeles High. I finally graduated with a 1.67 GPA. All of us children this time were headed out to Pomona, California. I was older now, so I could at least request visitation with my little sisters, including Nina who had been in foster care she was since two-months-old.

I visited Gena and Heather a couple of times with Tracy. We were placed in the Hunter family. The two boys were Lonnie and Lavell. They were real athletes. Basketball, football, and baseball. They were also popular. Tracy did not like it there, however. She wanted to leave. I also did, but I was tired of all the shuffling around. Mrs. Hunter assigned Tracy to so many chores that Tracy ran away. I tried to stay on a little longer so that I could continue my promise to look after my sisters as best I could. I was at the Hunters' foster home but did not blend well with them or the kids at school. One of Lonnie's buddies had a girlfriend named Janet Ballard. She was the little sister of the basketball star Greg Ballard. We liked each other, and we went on a couple of dates. Then I was jumped at school and beat up pretty bad, so I needed to get out of there. So, what did the social worker do next? They found Tracy, and we went right over to another foster home a few blocks away with a Mr. and Mrs. Benjamin. Tracy immediately did not like it because they just wanted her for household chores, and they only tolerated me. I was nearing the age that foster care parents were afraid of me. I did not understand it because I always carried myself as a sweet and kind person. Labeling and fear were standard in the foster care system. Tracy left, and I was there on my own. I still attended Ganesha High in Pomona, California. While at Ganesha High School, I had a brief introduction to high school football. There were many stars there that went on to play pro sports. I had the pleasure to briefly meet some in my travels. While at Ganesha High School, in addition to meeting the little sister of the phenom Greg Ballard, I was a schoolmate of George Hawthorne, the famous basketball star. He was the first seven-footer I had ever seen in real life. Big Dooney Williams, who started on varsity football as a sophomore, went on to college and played tight-end in the NFL.

The Benjamin's foster home was a teen experience. They were excessive gamblers and excessive drinkers. They would have their share of pass-out drunk battles. If I wanted something to eat, I was instructed to go in the kitchen and make it. I was fourteen and too old to be cooked for. I was hungry for many days because it seemed as though everything in the kitchen needed to be prepared. My very first cooking experience was a pork chop. I wanted a fried pork chop something terrible. I had grease getting hot in the pan. I put flour on the chops on both sides. I did not coat with eggs. The fire was too high. It cooked on the outside to the point of being burnt, but remained red and bloody on the inside. The whole house smelled burnt. When the Benjamins returned home, they showed me how to air out the house and the proper way to make a pork chop. I began learning how to prepare my meals.

They had some relatives on the other side of Pomona where they attended Gary High School. Over there was where I learned to hang out in the park like a gangster. I also took up drinking after being introduced to garage parties. Being there gave me a chance to visit my little sisters Gena and Heather in their foster home. Sometimes, I would show up drunk, and the foster father would get upset. I would be so drunk from Tickled Pink Boone's farm wine that after he verbally scolded me, I would sit on the curb out front, and he would bring Gena out, point at me and say, "Don't you grow up and be a loser like your brother over there, sitting on the curb."

I visited the Richie Family, some of the Benjamin's relatives. Tony, Renee, and Bennie were the oldest, and the young one was Ricky. I thought Renee was beautiful. I did not stay there much longer because my life was taking the path of a deviant teenager. It would be Tracy's and my last time at McClaren Hall. We made it clear that we did not want any more foster homes. I also remember not returning directly back to McClaren Hall. I was briefly placed in a cell for deviant youth offenders at the infamous Juvenile Hall. This was way out of my league. Major reputations floated around. I was very attentive here because I was utterly alone. Most people there were in a gang. The big names floating around were Tookie and Jamel. They were big-time Crips or gang-bangers. They usually worked out in groups. Tookie and Jamel were really buff dudes. I was not there for any crime; I was a political prisoner. It got me by. I was able to walk the grounds for an hour a day. I had a mattress, a toilet, and bunk alone in a room. I was there for a couple of weeks before getting shipped over to McClaren Hall and rejoining Tracy. No more foster homes. We were too old.

I spent the next few years in a boys' home in Riverside called Glen Ivey Boys Home. It was run, owned, and operated by the McClure family – Mr. McClure and his new, young wife. His ex-wife had a house close by. His son, Bobby McClure, was a counselor and surfer and had a house on the land. Glen Ivey was an old ranch orchard that was converted to a boys' home facility. The attempt there was to get me away from the inner-city ways that I was developing since my circumstances were different. The social workers and courts were beginning to realize that I was their creation. They were hiding me from my parents and at the same time, stopping me from heading down the wrong path. This boys' home was mostly for white kids. There were a couple Mexican kids, but everyone else was white, including the counselors. I still had a great experience.

I learned how to hike and camp, and we were allowed to go on many outings to the beach. One of the counselors, Mary, was a hippie with a Volkswagen who managed to take us to the beach and allowed us to gaze at her in her barely-fitting bikini, which was very sexy. Freddy, who was the oldest, seemed to get all the girls. He was close to eighteen. Steven Bazidlo was the first gay person I ever met. Boy, that guy was tough. He beat the sexist attitude I acquired right out of me. That dude could fight. We respected each other after that. I never really let on that I felt he got the best of me. I just made sure we were not in that predicament again. The art of survival.

I also learned how to catch snakes because the orchards were full of them. Gopher snakes and California king snakes that could beat diamond back rattlers. I would usually kill the rattlers on sight out of fear. I had a seven-year-old rattle I cut off myself. I also remember the fascination with the Los Angeles Rams at the boys home in Riverside. They loved the L.A. Rams because their roster at the time had the first black Rams quarterback, named James Harris. I became the overnight item because I was attending school at Norco Junior High and everyone was talking me up as being the black quarterback at Corona High School. Well, it never happened because I was shipped out of that home in Riverside to another home in a different school district.

I was eventually placed in a new boys' home in Inglewood when I was fifteen years old. This put me in a whole new environment than what I was used to because once you hit 15 years of age, you were placed with kids who had engaged in real criminal activity instead of runaways or kids who needed to be temporarily placed somewhere because their parents had done something. I would briefly go to McClaren Hall and then get shipped out to California Youth Homes in Inglewood, California. During the brief stay at McClaren Hall, I saw Tracy who was later sent to a girls' home. During that time I met Star. She was fast and furious. She catapulted me from regular black dude to big man. I would be shipped out to McClaren Hall, and Star stayed on as my girlfriend on the outside for a little while. She occasionally came to visit me. The boys' home took a toll on our relationship. First of all, I really was not one of them. These guys in this establishment were actual criminals and deviants. Drugs, money, and escapes were regular. The Latinos were into sniffing glue and paint in paper bags or socks. I tried it once or twice.

The Football romances. I began to love the game with time. There was a need for something to gravitate to and make me feel as if I was a winner or, at least, a loser with dignity. The boys' home Coach Harold Lloyd was also a counselor. He introduced me to my very first Fatburger, the first burger with an over-medium cooked egg and a hot link. One day after practice, Coach Lloyd took us to the first ever Fatburger stand in Los Angeles, which was nothing more than a shack on Jefferson and Western. Simply delicious.

During one of his visits, my father asked that I request Director Mike Linquatta to allow me to attend Los Angeles High School for my remaining time in the boys' home. I was hoping that I could recapture the possibility of getting a childhood education. I was allowed to attend public school, and I hoped I could correct my illiteracy. I was transferred out of the general unit of boys. In the Inglewood facility, there were probably 60 or 70 boys. I was shipped to Third and Normandy in Los Angeles to live in a group home. It housed six boys and some male and female counselors, some of whom were couples or even married. I was re-introduced to football by Coach Lloyd. I played on the defensive line. I was in the general population of the school in this boys home. All we did in school every day was shoot spitballs at each other, get into fights, and figure out ways to get high. Sometimes we sniffed paint and glue, but that was more common among the

Latino kids. I had lost my girlfriend Star (Estrella Mayo) to a couple of the gangsters in the general population. So, I had no problem leaving them and starting another chapter of my life. I was now living in the group home and attending Los Angeles High School.

Chapter 15

Los Angeles High School

I was placed in the second semester of eleventh grade. I was barely reading and writing, but that did not matter because I was allowed to attend public school away from the deviant children. I was feeling almost normal. It was beautiful. The school was rebuilt because the 1971 earthquake destroyed the old campus, where they filmed the TV show *Room 222*. It was called Walt Whitman High on TV. The school kept a memorial brass placard on display. Los Angeles High School was another environment where I saw black children with dreams and hopes. They were not about crime and seemed to have come from good family environments. Their dress to me appeared quite mature. I was again overwhelmed.

LA High had an impact on my social status. I met my crew – Kirk Kemp, Lavell Carter, and Michael Brown. It was lunchtime at school, and it was my very first lunch. Leaving class, one of the students said, "You better run so you can get a good spot in the lunch line." Many of us children were on the free lunch program. Many kids wanted to appear rich, so they had money to go get junk food or bring a spectacular meal. We four wound up together in the line. Those three had been at this same routine before my arrival. We hung out every day. We would walk around at breaks and at lunch. We shared likes and dislikes about females and campus issues. The guys all had a unique gimmick. I had none. Kirk was an artist. He was also the ladies' man. Lavell was in ROTC. He would wear his Army uniform every Friday. Lavell was also in the Rolling '60s Crips. The Crips were a dangerous gang. I would have never expected Lavell was that kind of person. He was the politest and most outspoken of the group. He greeted everyone. Teachers and security respected his personality. However, when school was out and Lavell went home, he was another guy.

Mike was a bookworm, or so I thought. He always had many books in his hand. I thought he always just buried himself into them. Well, that was not the case. He was just like us. The books just helped his personality because of the glasses. I think that was what made it look right. I needed a gimmick. I had nothing until I met Coach Williams. He saw a football player. He would approach me every day about coming out. I was not that good. I only got to play briefly. In CYH (California Youth Homes), he had a talk with Coach Harold Lloyd. In fact, Coach Lloyd and I would remain friends through my football days at California State University, Northridge. I also came back to the boys' home to participate in a staff vs. student game while I was attending college. I was an ambassador of hope for those other kids. The Director, Mike Linquata, also played in the staff vs. student game. Mike Linquatta was the reason I was on the right track then. On one of my father's visits, my dad asked if I could attend public school. I went directly to Mike Linquatta and pitched my request. My reasoning was very descriptive. I told him that all we did in school was spit paper balls at each other through straws, adding that the curriculum was not

Graduation from Los Angeles High School on June 13, 1979

challenging. I became a test for the future of the establishment. After me, several more children were permitted to attend public school. Even though I was now in Los Angeles High School, my family's situation remained the same.

Chapter 16

Clamentha Steward

Tracy, Gena, Heather, and I were still in the system. Mike, Verna, Mom, and Dad were staying with a lovely lady named Mrs. Clamentha Steward. I would get to visit on weekends from time to time. Our parents were still in the fight for case #895188. On those visiting days, we slept in a backroom foldout couch, and my parents were in a living room on the floor. I know this was terrible for Verna and Michael because they had to endure living in the car with our folks before meeting Mrs. Stewart. I remember what it was like to live on the streets. For a brief period before Inglewood, we lived on Skid Row. I slept on a park bench in the middle of the day sometimes. We would spend the day hanging out in Persian Square in downtown Los Angeles. People lived in shopping carts. We were living in a studio-turned-hotel overlooking Persian Square that someone put us up in. Grand Hotel food was delicious. We lived off mini-donations and sometimes family assistance programs.

I remember back when I was playing a football game for the boys' home. The results of the staff game probably would have been different if big Aquilla Jackson was still there. I believe we had to cancel one of our Catholic high school opponent's games because they found out that he reached age 19, which disqualified him from playing against children. Back when I lived there, Aquilla Jackson was the leader of the boys. I never thought he was 18 or 19 years old; I thought he was about 40 years old. He stood at about 6'6" and was built like George Forman. He was an actual pimp. He was the only pimp I had ever met and had conversations with. The staff gave him many privileges. He had grown women paying him weekend visits, and they would leave the boys home for the weekend. I was not really hip to that part of the institutional operations. My focus was to get into public school and onto a different track in life.

From the age of 4 years old to age 57, something was always trying to pull me back into the crab pot. I had to resist. I played on the staff football team against the boys' home football team called the Knights without Aquilla Jackson. They were an eight-man team. They played against small schools and Catholic schools. I played for them a couple of years before, when I was still a terrible player. I was number 42. I learned not to quit and keep fighting. I learned how to give 100%, especially if I wanted to play. Otherwise, it was a long game from the sidelines with a terrible view. Some jokes you would hear were: riding pine, bench warmer, cheer squad, etc. The atmosphere could be brutal. In the end, I knew my dad enjoyed football; it was his entertainment, and I finally understood why he appreciated it so much.

My illiteracy stopped me in my tracks. I left the boys' home and went straight to college. I was not prepared. I would also experience the same difficulty in the Navy evaluations because of the same illiteracy issues. After a certain point, advancement in the Navy as a career path became difficult. The Navy was a great experience for a kid without a path, did not want to go to jail, wanted to learn some independence and discipline, and put life in perspective. I realized my limitations in learning due to lack of preparation and other roadblocks. The Navy was going to be a new beginning for me, a new life away from the institutions and the foster care system and jumping from home to home with my parents' struggles. I was going to separate my past from wherever I was headed in the future.

Chapter 17

Cal State University Northridge

Before the Navy, I enrolled at California State University of Northridge. My real parents helped me move into the dorm. They even accompanied me to the meeting with the Dean. This is where I should have first noticed my illiteracy if I ever had been able to figure that out myself. Everything at this point in my life was not accomplished by me. In January of 1979 when Los Angeles High School had all of us fill out applications to three schools, I did as instructed. I was totally clueless, could barely read and write, and had the intellect of a seventh grader, while all my peers seemed to be on track as seniors. They all had dreams. It was as if they had been planning on moving on for a long time. I was just there. I was finally in public school but was not ready to leave high school.

Before the Navy, I enrolled at California State University of Northridge. My real parents helped me move into the dorm. They even accompanied me to the meeting with the Dean. This was where my illiteracy could no longer be ignored and I was faced with the realization that I had accomplished nothing in my life. In January of 1979 when Los Angeles High School had all of us fill out applications to three schools, I did as instructed. I was totally clueless, could barely read and write, and had the intellect of a seventh grader, while all my peers seemed to be on track as seniors. They all had dreams. It was as if they had been planning on moving on for a long time. I was stuck there. I was finally in public school but was not ready to leave high school.

Lavell and I were seniors. Kirk and Mike were juniors, so they had another year. Luckily, I scored high on the SAT. I was exceptionally high in the math portions; English and writing were terrible. I was really enjoying Los Angeles High School. I must give credit to Mr. Jones, the algebra teacher, for his strict rules and the way he firmly dealt with cocky and mouthy boys. Individually, if you went up and worked a problem out on the board, he ensured you knew how to do it. There was not enough time for everyone to work the chalkboard in that hour, but he knew who needed it. I thought he was hard on me to set an example, since I was from a boys' home. Honestly, the way I dressed in those days was gangster. I wore whatever I could get my hands on – mostly canvas shoes and khaki pants. They were the only clothes to trade with the other boys in the boys' home. I did not have parents around to tell me when to get a haircut, so I wore whatever big afro I could reach and a pick fork in my hair.

Anyway, I turned 18 on June 13, 1979, and I graduated high school the same day.

I was legally released from the boys' home, although I was allowed to stay until August of 1979. My parents were still controlling my every move, all the way down to where the financial aid was going. They made sure that what was left over was contributed to the Leon and Esther fund. The excess money was gathered for my parents and my older siblings to purchase a family home where

Gena and Heather could complete their childhood undisturbed by case #895188.

Once again, on the new college campus, I was catapulted into another dimension, a higher level of black children. I was so far behind. My parents made promises to the Dean of Engineering on my behalf that I was never able to fulfill. My dad practically picked my degree for me. I could never do what I wanted; he had to control every aspect of my life. He was not even the person who raised me. I was in a battle of respect, hate, and new freedom, but there was a cost. I never really got released. I was in captivity from transition to transition. I was learning to resent my father. It had been burning for a long time inside. I also began to view the two of them, my mother and father, as evil. Two self-serving people that only cared about their own gripes and concerns.

I observed how involved they were now with Gena and Heather's education and future. My sister Tracy was slowly getting driven to prison by my parent's manipulation. My sister Tracy sent everyone in our immediate family a one-million-dollar check issued by Key Bank. Tracy wound up serving a prison sentence for fraud. She was influenced by my parents. I had to stand by and observe the continuous battered abuse of my eldest brother Michael, who could not even use his own judgment. If my eldest brother did not nod his head in agreement with my father, he would take one across the face. If he did not utter the correct response, then he would take another one across the face. The day I lost total respect for my father was when I said I was joining the Navy. I took one across the jaw for wanting to free myself from them. Their mental captivity was worse than any place that I had ever been. I began to only see a side of my parents that was evil and self-serving.

I was doing pretty well in the first year of college. I enjoyed some of the classes, and I was learning things. My social side was failing miserably. I was way over my head. The class work began to require more reading and more work. I was trying to keep up, but I was weak. Before college, I never really had to commit myself to study. I never had to commit myself to accomplishing anything. What would make school work any different?

The dorm was very exciting. The students were so far ahead because they had good study habits, but they seemed to be able to partake in all the campus and dorm festivities. The parties, joining fraternities, and going home on the weekend... They had the support of family and friends, and all the fundamentals and prerequisites needed to succeed in school. I, on the other hand, did not. Although I tried to do what they did, every semester my GPA was slipping, and I got warnings and threats that my money would be cut off. Once my parents helped me to transition from boys' home and high school into college and got their cut of that substantial initial installment, I was on my own.

I was approaching my second year, and the money allowances were rolling in on schedule as long as my grades were above 2.0 GPA. My parents subtracted their cut for the house. I could not even maintain a 2.0 GPA, but I did something I felt would improve my social game. I had absolutely no financial game because college took all the money my parents did not need. I had joined the California State Northridge University football team and was living in a teammate's spare room. I walked on, made the team, and really felt like somebody. The boys' home was proud of me. Coach Harold Lloyd and Director Mike Linquatta were proud of me. That was how I managed to go back and play in the high school vs. staff game. At the same time, I was neglecting my studies and I never really established a study regimen. Back in the dorms, I began to fall into the crowd that did not have to study as often.

Football practice and studying engineering were more than I could bear. During this time at State, I had the opportunity to meet Barack Obama, the 44th President of the United States. Ron Lewis, the son of the Dean Lewis of Hamilton High School, was also attending Cal. St. Northridge and was one of the coolest brothers in the dorms. There were many. One day, back in 1981, we were hanging out around Ron Lewis' dorm room when this skinny, light-skinned dude from Pepperdine College walked into the dorm room to meet Ron. He was introduced as "Barack Obama," and several of us began to snicker. Yukking it up over his name, we all kind of gave some funny little snickers and then someone asked, "Barack?" He replied, "Just call me Barry." So, that's what we called him. Little did I ever imagine he would one day become POTUS #44. Whatever we did is between us and POTUS#44. We left the room because he was there to see Carl. We hung out for a minute and moved on. I did not smoke with POTUS either; we left the room to give them some privacy. It was a brief encounter that I would probably never have remembered if he had not become President of the United States.

In my sophomore year at the university, I had the pleasure of meeting many of the students in the dorms. Since I had no study regimen, I spent a lot of time after football practice wandering the halls of the dorms with other students who liked to look for fun. Ron Lewis had the reputation and the popularity. He was ahead of all of us. He was making money. That is all I will say in that area. But, he also had the goods. I hit the joint once there.

The last major experience I had while attending CSUN and playing football for them was the opportunity to play on National Television. CSUN was a Division II school. Some of the colleges liked to schedule a guaranteed victory for their homecoming games. CSUN was scheduled to play The University of Reno, Nevada, a Division I school. They had a premier running back, Frank Hawkins. This was a beast of a man. In fact, their whole team seemed to be twice our size. I loved every minute of the brief notoriety, complete with interviews, cameras, and momentary stardom. Toward the second half of the game, the defensive line coach was telling us linemen to just lay down so that the linebackers could see and make more tackles. Those Reno-Nevada linemen had their way with us. My most significant and most infamous moment was running to the sideline to tackle big Frank Hawkins, who laid me out with a stiff arm and then scored on national television. I hated it. I was embarrassed about it for a long time, but now it is a great story to tell. I was eventually able to redeem some self-esteem.

I also had a group of friends in the dorm that were more beach bums. They were not particularly popular. They were not bookworms or geniuses. They did the minimum required to succeed and knew the degree they wanted was attainable for them. I was the one out of my league with engineering. These guys wanted to perform in a dorm talent contest. This was before karaoke. We were actually singing. We worked for two weeks, and one of the girls in the dorm gave me voice training because everyone said I was terrible. When she finished, I was singing "My Girl" so well I could have gotten a record deal. There were five of us, and we did short sections of songs a Capella style. I opened our rendition that night and we received a standing ovation. Another fantastic college experience.

It was in the middle of my sophomore year, on academic probation, that I realized I had exhausted everything I could do in college. I was out of my league. The classes that required reading, writing, and comprehension were taking their toll on me. I could not pretend anymore about my skillset. I was undisciplined and had no real study routine. I could not write a complete sentence. I could not hold a moderate level conversation. The coach offered me a partial scholarship because he had heard that I was starving and failing, but by then in my mind, it was too late.

I went to a theater in Hollywood the next day. I was sitting in the theater ready to watch a movie called *Stripes*. It was a great movie. It was about changing your life and making a big move when things are just not going right. I left that movie and walked into a Navy recruiter's office. I told him that I wanted to join and I wanted to join now. The recruiter said, "Not so fast, let's find you a career or a job." I took this long test with many areas of testing. I scored high in the mathematical exercises. I was not writing or comprehending well, but I read well enough to get accepted into the fire control electronics program. I was also given other choices, but the recruiter said that this field was looking for more minorities that were attracted to the electronics field. I was excited. I really felt like I was not that far behind after all. I just needed a new direction.

I broke the news to my parents that evening, but things did not go too well. My dad caught me off guard with a right hook. I was startled and shocked at the same time. Then anger started burning deep inside of me. I was stunned and angry, which made me that much more eager to join the Navy. I wanted to leave. I was living at the house that my older brothers and sister were able to purchase through the organizational skills of my parents and whatever they used of my financial aid money. My parents were in complete control. The home was really huge. An old craftsman three story home located in South Central Los Angeles. I left one type of controlled atmosphere for another. None of that would get me to stay any longer. I was 20 years old. I had been living this nightmare of a life for twenty years. Young and lacking any other options, I never thought about the ramifications of my actions. I was destabilized from the age of 4 until my release from the Los Angeles Department of Social Services at age 18. Unprepared for a college education, I headed for boot camp.

Chapter 18

The Military

I realized while riding the bus to San Diego that I was ready for whatever I was facing. The guys with me were also going to be in my boot camp company. Upon arrival, we were given clothing and boots while we bagged up everything we owned. At first, everyone in a uniform seemed to enjoy yelling and barking orders and rules. We took showers and got dressed. We were immediately shown to our bunks, and at night we were instructed to go to bed. It honestly felt as though I had just laid my head down to go to sleep when the noise began. The officers stormed in banging on trash cans and trash can lids, yelling "Up, up and at 'em, Reveille," rolling whole trash cans down the middle of the barracks. Everything they did was to generate the most unexpected and disturbing loud noise, and these dudes really loved it. This would continue over and over until we were up and in formation. Then the Company Commander went over the rules and regulations.

The first march which was very sloppy at first, right to the chow hall for breakfast. In the chow hall, I learned to eat fast and then get back out to formation. For the next eight weeks, I marched, ran, ate, learned, cleaned, marched, and ran again. We did all this over and over for a graduation colors competition; Navy boot camp companies were competing in marching and formations against other Navy boot camp companies. Across the fence in San Diego, the Marines were doing the same competitions for their graduation ceremonies.

Each night when I went to bed after a day of marching and push-ups, I dozed off thinking of the movie Stripes and all of the traveling I would be doing to other countries. The illiterate guy was easily influenced, and when two weeks passed in boot camp, I found myself joining the smoking circle because the smoking circle guys got smoking breaks when things got a little rough. Aside from picking up the smoking habit, the physical part of boot camp was enjoyable, and I felt good to actually achieve something challenging. I would continue to seek challenges and excitement the whole time I served, which ended with an Honorable Discharge. The reading and the need to comprehend and absorb all the information they wanted me to know was very difficult. I was learning everything and passing all the tests and marching, and I was even very competitive in running the mile and a half in 12 minutes. Everything was going great for me in boot camp. I was going to be advanced to Seaman upon graduation for the college credits I acquired at California State. Until the last two weeks of boot camp. Ugh. The load was just too much for me to bear. I was memorizing, running, and studying; we had some side duties, and I was just plain tired. I failed the second before the last weekly exam along with 14 other guys, and we had to attend the infamous marching party. The marching party was brutal. It went on more than four hours. I ran, and we marched and did push-ups with our M-14 rifles and helmets. On many of the counts, the rifle was stretched out over our heads at arm's length. Brutal. Then we had to retake the test, pass it, and pass the final with the rest of the company on time for graduation and ceremony.

I managed to make it through up to the last test, but I was not alone: all 14 of us failed. We were called the Lucky 14. The punishment was a grueling three hours in full gear and rifle while attending a marching party. After that, we passed the tests and were now officially allowed to graduate boot camp.

Liberty weekend! We stepped out of the gate in our cracker-jack uniforms. I was with four of my graduation buddies, and while hailing a cab, a trio of prostitutes headed our direction. The one in the middle was an ex-girlfriend who had dumped me back while I was in the California youth boys home. I was dating Estrella Mayo "Star" back at McClaren Hall, and then, I transferred out to California Youth Homes for boys in Inglewood California across from Centinela Park. Well, I ran into Star again. She was very sexy and beautiful after all this time. We didn't recognize one another at first, just engaged in some conversation and I finally realized the voice was hers. She then recognized me and acknowledged that we had dated in the past, and she began to walk away. I called out to her to come back. "I just want to talk to you!" I ran after her saying, "Hey, Star! It's me, Darryl. I want you to talk to me," but she kept walking and jerking her shoulder away. The only thing I can think of was that she might have been too embarrassed to face me. Sometimes I would see her again on various corners in San Diego, but there was never any conversation again. I just wanted to see if there was anything that I could do to better her situation. The way she and I broke up back at the boy's home was very rude. Those few guys laughed at me for a couple of weeks. Now I know why. They knew this about her, and I had no idea. Anyway, that first graduation weekend was spectacular. I could not go home to my parents because I was in a drunken stupor for the whole weekend, and we did not want to report back in late. Three of us went in on a motel and purchased a lot of alcohol, and the party was festive: young and older girls, and whatever else you could do in San Diego, CA.

It was there in San Diego in basic electronic school where my friends from boot camp began to pass electronic tracks ahead of me. My very first school after boot camp was BEEP (Basic Electricity and Electronics Program) school. I was so behind scholastically that I would continue to be set back and repeat tracks for several additional weeks. I did well in some specific areas. Then, there were areas that I would get hung up on. Transistor theory was an area I had to do over three times. Eventually, I moved on, buckled down, and passed.

Company members who moved on earlier than I did went on to their "A" school. Like me, those who found the curriculum challenging and were left behind, remained in San Diego and would move on to their respective destinations when they passed. I was still in San Diego completing tracks of the basic electricity program. My first setback was dropping out of college. I was not prepared. I took another detour for the military, then I had trouble in boot camp with testing and joining the Lucky 14. Now I repeated several weeks to complete a basic electricity and electronics program because of the math problems.

After taking more time than most, I finally graduated from the basic electricity and electronics program. I was happy to be leaving San Diego and headed to Great Lakes Naval Base in northern

Illinois, very near the Wisconsin border. I had only heard stories and rumors about Wisconsin, but the coolest thing about the state was that the drinking age was just 19 years. It was at this time that I met my first drinking girlfriend, a blonde who was also in the Navy. In the Navy, we addressed each other by our last name. I only remember her last name was Wolcott like the boxer Jersey Joe Wolcott. We played lots of pool in our off-hours and went drinking. It was cold in this part of the country, and for me, the school curriculum was demanding once again. Ron Stanosek was one of my friends and troop member of the Lucky 14 in boot camp and now a Fire Controlman. He was from Germantown, Wisconsin and was a cool and brilliant dude. He helped me with some instruction when I was having trouble. All I could think of was how close I was getting to the point of travel just like in *Stripes*, where I would be able to see the world. I had to move to Great Lakes to attend the Fire Control Electronics class "A" school. In 12 weeks, I would be on a ship. By week three, I began repeating tracks; if not one week, then it would be two weeks. Twelve weeks of school turned into eight months. I finally graduated with a class of guys that graduated boot camp long after me. That was fine. I got used to the idea early. The faces never stayed the same for long. I met so many people in passing that I knew I better get used to it. I got orders to my first ship USS Biddle CG-34. I would be stationed in Norfolk, Virginia. The East Coast became the new frontier. I had never been to the East Coast.

and uncle served in WWII; many blacks were there. In the Navy, there were many blacks in WWII, but they could only do certain jobs. However, as time passed, things slowly improved. My uncle was an extraordinary case – a Navy dentist. They would allow black professionals in the medical and dental profession so the white doctors did not have to treat the black patients. There were a limited number of black doctors and dentists to perform that work. For many years, a black guy could only do service work: cooking, cleaning, sweeping, and swabbing. Needless to say, the advanced electronics fields were the slowest. There I was for a couple of months without anyone firmly representing me in my corner. I was also the lowest-ranked person. The next black person was my first Chief; his name was Chief Seals. He was a great example of a man that went through it to make it. We had to come to an understanding. He was a new Chief who also had to prove himself. The dynamics of color, respect, and competitions of intelligence was always lingering in the air. Many of these guys were at the top of their class.

I stated earlier that the boatswain mates were in the compartment above me and many boatswain's mates were predominately black sailors. Keep in mind Chief-Boats was one of the most essential members onboard. All shipboard maneuvers and preservation are accomplished because of the boatswain mates. I met and hung out with many of those guys, especially Seaman Eddie Brown. Eddie had a slick, brown Camaro, and he was a good friend. We had a lot of fun in Virginia, the North Atlantic, the Black Sea region, the Mediterranean Sea, and the Indian Ocean. Don't get me wrong; everybody got along for the most part. Things got crazy sometimes, but the ship is mostly family, especially overseas.

There I was, stationed on board the USS Biddle CG-34. Unfortunately, I was not one of the prize fire-control technicians. The prize fire control technicians were the 6-year, class "C" school graduates. They were automatically advanced to E-4, Third Class

Petty Officer, at the completion of school before ever making it to the ship.

Stationed at NOB, I was standing watch aboard the USS Biddle CG-34 in Director Five, which it was called is the rangefinder of the Mark 68 Gunfire Control System. It was my baby. I kept it clean and performed 3-M (maintenance, material, management) in it. When overseas, I stood or sat watch in the Director. It was a box-type unit that housed the rangefinder which sat high above the gun mount positioned on a higher level of the ship. I had to run to this box whenever an alarm sounded, day or night. Sometimes getting to this place required me to respond quickly. I may have to run up several ladders or jump through a scuttle (circular doors and hatches through-out ship) or two or more.

I was a pretty big guy by Navy standards. I usually carried weight at a maximum of my weight parameters. I was 6 feet tall, so my maximum weight was 221 pounds. My life living onboard ship and whenever we would hit a port was running. I was determined to always compete at the top of the qualification chart. I always wanted to contribute physically because of what I lacked scholastically, so I always found myself volunteering for extra labor.

Chapter 19

The Conservative East Coast Navy

My new state, Virginia, was where my mother was born. I was stationed at Norfolk Ordinance Base (NOB), aboard the USS Biddle CG-34 as a Fire Control Technician Guns. My first contract with the Navy was a "3 by 6," meaning that I owed three years of active duty service and three years in reserve inactive. I loved the new experience. I was assigned a compartment with the fire-control technicians and the gunner's mates, which was understandable because the gunner's load the weapons that the fire-control technicians guided and controlled in the line of fire. The compartment, or sleeping quarters, were at the forward end of the ship called the bow. I was assigned a top bunk. Junior guys get the top, the worst bunk possible. Once I packed in, and I lived in it for a while, it became home and hard to want to move, although eventually, for a better bunk, you will move. The boatswain mates were in the compartment above me. This is relevant because of the situation at the testing station, where I trained to get into the Navy. They needed minorities in the advanced electronics field. I first arrived at the fire control technician's department as the only black guy. Actually, from the start of boot camp through BEEP school and "A" school, I met only one black guy. That was in 1982.

In the '60s, the numbers were even lower for minorities. My dad and uncle were among many blacks who served in WWII. In the Navy, during WWII, blacks could only do certain jobs. However, as time passed, things slowly improved. My uncle was an extraordinary case – a Navy dentist. They would allow black professionals in the medical and dental profession so the white doctors did not have to treat the black patients. There were a limited number of black doctors and dentists to perform that work. For many years, a black guy could only do service work: cooking, cleaning, sweeping, and swabbing. Needless to say, the advanced electronics fields were the slowest. There I was, for a couple of months, without anyone firmly representing me in my corner. I was also the lowest-ranked person. The next black person was my first Chief; his name was Chief Seals. He was a great example of a man that went through it to make it. We had to come to an understanding. He was a new Chief who also had to prove himself. The dynamics of color, respect, and competitions of intelligence were always lingering in the air. Many of these guys were at the top of their class, and were not lightweights.

I stated earlier that the boatswain mates were in the compartment above me and many boatswain's mates were predominately black sailors. Keep in mind Chief-Boats were some of the most essential members onboard. All shipboard maneuvers and preservation are accomplished because of the boatswain mates. I met and hung out with many of those guys, especially Seaman Eddie Brown. Eddie had a slick, brown Camaro, and he was a good friend. We had a lot of fun in Virginia, the North Atlantic, the Black Sea region, the Mediterranean Sea, and the Indian Ocean. Don't get me wrong, everybody got along for the most part. Things got crazy sometimes, but the ship is mostly family, especially overseas.

There I was, stationed on board the USS Biddle CG-34. Unfortunately, I was not one of the prize fire-control technicians. The prize fire control technicians were the 6-year, class "C" school graduates. They were automatically advanced to E-4, Third Class Petty Officer, at the completion of school before ever making it to the ship.

Stationed at NOB, I was standing watch aboard the USS Biddle CG-34 in Director Five, which is the rangefinder of the Mark 68 Gunfire Control System. It was my baby. I kept it clean and performed 3-M duties (maintenance, material, management) on it. When overseas, I stood or sat watch in the Director. It was a box-type unit that housed the rangefinder which sat high above the gun mount positioned on a higher level of the ship. I had to run to this box whenever an alarm sounded, day or night. Sometimes getting to this place required me to respond quickly. I may have to run up several ladders or jump through a scuttle (circular doors and hatches through-out ship) or two or more.

I was a pretty big guy by Navy standards. I usually carried weight at the maximum of my weight range. I was 6 feet tall, so my maximum weight was 221 pounds. My spare time onboard ship and whenever we would hit a port was spent running. I was determined to always compete at the top of the qualification chart. I always wanted to contribute physically because of what I lacked scholastically, so I always found myself volunteering for extra labor.

Chapter 20

Made Me Weak at the Knees

Cold starts were the physical requirement tests that would happen after weeks of not being able to train because of the conditions. Over the years, the banging up and down the ladders, the jumps through the scuttles, and the cold starts caused my knees to swell, and the doctor would recommend limited duty. Each doctor onboard every ship would make a medical entry about my knees, but most times, the low man status was hard to relinquish. So, it was usually more important for me to stay healthy and stay onboard the ship. It was important for me to have the Navy's seal stamped on my medical records. The doctor told me to keep some copies for myself because I would have trouble with my knees later in life.

Another adventure that a low-ranking member of a division like myself had to participate in was kitchen duty. For three months, I was sent to work for the cook (called K-P duty in the Army and other branches). I started in the scullery, then the machines that washed the dishes, glasses, silverware, and trays. I worked in this area for a couple of weeks with guys dispersed from other departments. From the scullery, I was moved over to the deep sink, the area to scrub the big pots and pans caked with burnt grit usually an inch thick. The cooks did not wash dishes or pots and pans.

In the deep sink area, the water was scalding hot, and I wore huge rubber gloves, alone for a couple of hours after every meal scrubbing them clean. I liked this job because I worked alone and was not interrupted to do another task elsewhere. This is not to say the cooks did not work hard, they did. Three to four meals a day for a thousand people and this was a smaller ship. There were bigger ships with 5000 people. Cooks would get new shipboard members like me every three months to help out, clean the kitchen, and support the general organization of the mess hall. After the scullery, I was assigned to another area, and it would be my last assignment on kitchen duty. I was sent upstairs to serve the officers who had their own cooks and a different menu. The food was prepared restaurant style. I was shown how to serve with elegance. I was taught how tables were formally set: salad forks, butter knives, steak knives, spoons just for soup. There was a particular side to pour water or serve seconds. There were to be no comments or facial expressions. I had some of the best food, like fried chicken; it was not just crusted, but had a special herb batter, deep fried, and served with candy roasted carrots and cauliflower. Delicious. The cooks were that good.

Kitchen duty was also an excellent way to make friends and set up future deals and favors. I could make arrangements with food to get laundry favors. Sometimes you may want your own load of clothes done separately, like your civilian clothing. You could also learn how to loan shark your money to increase your income. The average rate was 20 for 30. For example, if you lent someone 20 bucks, then the very next payday, they would have to pay 30. It was a nice way to make an extra 100 to 200 bucks a month, although, sometimes you got stiffed. That was when it became problematic. You wouldn't go and fight the person, which some guys made the mistake of doing. That only got both of you in trouble with a restriction to the ship and a fine. The best way to handle getting stiffed was with patience. You'd wait until they really needed you again. The word would spread that this person is a problem. When they needed you again, which they almost always did, you would deny them any money. If you did give in, the price would be worse. Instead of 20 for 30, the new rate would be 20 for 40 plus, collateral.

There were several duties to do besides your regular job. There were some duty days where you stood four-hour watches on guard duty. I was assigned to firefighting units, and I went to shipboard firefighting school. I was also trained as Security Alert Force/ Back-up Alert Force (SAF/BAF). This was our main side duty. We were the weapons guys, the gunner's mates, and the fire control technicians. We were called the Gunner's. I learned how to shoot a 45-caliber gun, 50-caliber machine gun, and M-14 rifles. I learned how to take them apart and put them back together. I learned how to throw a grenade over the side of the ship.

The best way to survive day to day aboard the ship was to be pleasant, patient, and mind your business. Everyone, for the most part, had a sense of humor: dry humor, mean humor, prankster humor, insulting humor, then the one without a funny bone at all. While I was gracious to all the ethnicities on board ship, I wanted to gravitate towards the black guys. I was fascinated because for most of my life inside of these institutions and foster homes, black people were the lower side of society. Every time I arrived somewhere different from the life I had endured, I found that the black people had a different motivation. Their motivation was not crime-driven. Los Angeles High School, Cal State – Northridge, and now the United States Navy, the black people had ambition, harbored plans on achievement, communicated well, had hopes and dreams. This was all new to me. I was simply overwhelmed.

This realization left me feeling that I was so far behind that I needed to do a lot to catch up with regard to my maturity level. I was socially inept because of the environments that I had been accustomed to. This is where I stopped thinking and talking in groups that I felt were above my limitations. I became isolated. I realized that I needed to read and learn in order to contribute. I needed to learn how to articulate my thoughts better because these people all around me had the education I lacked.

The compartment above me on the ship, where the boatswain mates lived, had a significant number of black guys. I fit in with them. I found that the school systems across the country failed black people. I saw that in the Navy. Brown vs. Board of Education took its toll on my parents and my family. These black guys were from different places all around the country. We were that group of blacks out of the '60s and '70s that were introduced to busing and desegregating the school systems, the group that had minimal scholastic supplies. They were cool, and being a boatswain mate was an excellent craft if that was what you wanted to do. Most of these guys were from the South and the East with a mixed bag of dreams. Not many of the blacks in that division really wanted to be a boatswain mate. Most were studying or applying to ship to another job. For me, they were guys I could hang out with onboard the ship to escape from the usual daily routine. Guys would tell jokes and make fun of how a night out on liberty was full of hysterical laughter. Sometimes, the guys would even talk trash to each other, and folks standing around would just be laughing like they were hearing some stand-up comedy routine. Many days were laughter-filled.

I needed to make educational changes, so I began to work on myself. I was Rangefinder Tracker then. The rangefinder telescope allowed me to see the landing of the Mark 68-gun fire control system round (bullet) while I was on the coast of Beirut, Lebanon. Circling from Israel and back again, I watched them trade fire with Israel night after night, day after day aboard ship. During these watches, I knew I wasn't reading and comprehending at a level that I should be, so I started reading as much as I could. Usually, when I read a page of a book, nothing would register. It just seemed that I was only good at making out sounds of words and that allowed me to sound as if I had some education. In actuality, I had no comprehension of what I read. I began reading Western novels with usually about a hundred pages. I liked the thin books at first so that I would not feel overwhelmed. There was something about the width of the book that made me feel I could accomplish reading the entire book. What drew me to read even more was the lonely cowboy. He would grow in these books and take on a challenge. Some were also very vivid in the sexual descriptions that made the reading more interesting. The sexual innuendos pulled me into the novel, and a little gun-fighting kept me going.

From there, I began moving on to bigger novels like *The Hotel New Hampshire,* and *The World According to Garp.* I enjoyed John

Irving novels because I got used to the way he wrote. Then I moved on to more educational readings about history, philosophy, the civil rights movement, and present day events. During that time, illiteracy had a way of affecting advancement in positions, communication skills around the water cooler, and any other questions posed to me in conversations that would determine if I was equal to my peers.

Advancement in the military is based on evaluation and conduct and what one learned while serving. Several years later, when I was reading over some of my earlier assessments and had learned how to read and comprehend, I saw the reason for my demise. Keywords were emphasized that paint a picture of someone's weaknesses. How you were graded and what was written about you followed you throughout your career. It will either make or break you. One cannot underestimate the importance of a fair and equitable education.

The USS Biddle CG-34 was where I began my quest for knowledge. The problem was catching up because I was so far behind. While onboard in 1986, I had a three-month deployment through the North Atlantic Ocean and the Black Sea Region. This cruise was a diplomacy venture. Several things were happening in this region of the world that required the presence of our ships, and the ship crew would need to pay close attention. A few countries had just broken away from the USSR, and several diplomatic ties from the past were in the midst of changing hands. The most I had seen of Africa was the coastal region to the west, heading up towards Gibraltar. Our ship anchored out and we took small crafts to shore. We were spreading democracy, which I thought meant helping the countries that were suffering, and it was great. I was seeing different people and places.

The cuisine was absolutely delicious. I mean, the food was cooked in these huge ceramic pots, and I sat on the rug to eat. I ate with bread scooping the sauce after wrapping the meat. Thinking back about the surroundings in Gibraltar, there was a mixture of religious beliefs and cultural foods in big pots. I saw many different types of clothing, turbans, and a few of the men wearing those fez hats, like on *Seinfeld*. From there, we traveled up through the North Atlantic to Spain. I met two drop-dead gorgeous Spanish female twins on the Island of Palma de Majorca, Spain. The Island was beautiful with colorful flowers and trees. The nightclub was very welcoming to us. They loved Americans and treated me well. In Naples, Italy, I met the famous hooker named "Humpty Dumpty." I rode my first double-decker bus in Scotland, and in Ireland I stumbled out of bars where it was so foggy that I could not see my hand at arm's length. I went through a tour of Edinburgh Castle long before getting addicted to the hit HBO series Game of Thrones.

I enjoyed England and stopping and visiting port after port through the English straits. After leaving the North Atlantic, our ship cautiously traveled through the Black Sea. Adversarial nation ships were all around us. There was a code of ship conduct going through these areas, especially when passing Russian ships. Many times, our ships would turn silent, and all hands head below decks. Our mission was to observe the people of Yugoslavia and Romania. These two countries had just broken away from the Soviet Union, and war had just taken place. With what had happened, our purpose over there was to show support and render assistance to the Balkan countries that were suffering. Our ship went to Yugoslavia after their battle for independence from the

USSR. In Romania, I was sitting across from Romanian military men. We really only nodded or waved because of the language barrier. We were respectful towards each other with our medals on our chest and machismo on display.

Walking through these cities and countries, I sensed the sadness. There were long lines where people would pick up bread and dry goods on certain days and dairy on others. We were also there to ensure safeguards for the children who were dismembered and disabled, suffering abuse and neglect. The aftereffects of war were ugly, and I had not even been to war yet. We returned back to Virginia, and it was not long before heading out to my first American cruise engaged in conflict. On board the USS Biddle CG-34, I cruised the Mediterranean Sea and the Indian Ocean for six months. This time, I was traveling as a fire control technician, no more side-duty jobs that would take me entirely out of the task. I had two years of schooling to be prepared for the team.

I was now learning the job of Director Five Tracker, up above the gun-mount controlling the line of fire of the 5-inch-round shells. That was a powerful gun shell we usually used for shore bombardment and sometimes for anti-air, but they were way too slow. The guns were mainly for firing upon other ships, but in this day and age, we should never be that close. There were a few skirmishes, which allowed me to collect a few medals along the way. The decorations I received included the Armed Forces Expeditionary Medal, the Battle E medal, and Navy Expeditionary medal. We stopped for gun training and coordination drills with the Army, Navy, and Marine GITMO personnel. GITMO was an island around Cuba where we attacked and blew up targets. I became pretty good as a Director 5 Rangefinder Tracker. I gave latitude and longitudinal corrections in mils (the measures on the scale in the scope) for the gunfire control system to hit on-target. I had a lot of pressure on me because I knew that I would probably be the first to die if hit up in that box. This position made all the compartment jokes down below decks. I could see the attacking planes coming right at me, then take a sudden turn. The visuals were great, like giant binoculars. I would just ignore them and give the system the best spots that I could deliver. I also received hazardous duty pay for this dangerous assignment. Our ship headed over to the Mediterranean Sea and the Indian Ocean for that six-month deployment. Our country was not at war. The world police were always on duty.

While making a circle between Israel and Beirut, Lebanon, I manned the rangefinder from 8 pm to 8 am, the night shift, for over 44 days, watching missiles going back and forth in complete terror every night. Eventually, the rockets became a normal occurrence to me. The rangefinder allowed me to feel like I was right there in the thick of the battle while most of the ship was tucked away in their comfy racks. The duty officer that was supposed to be up there with me liked to show up for drills after an enemy acquisition or exercises conducted during the day. Overnight, the Weapons Officer preferred being in his comfy bed. A couple of times, he would show up at night if the ship went to General Quarters – when the whole ship mans their respective battle stations. Since we were off the coast for over 44 days, the entire ship was allowed two beers each. I sold mine for 20 dollars per beer.

Heading back the United States, we were sidetracked over to Granada to support the rescue of some students. I picked up another medal for that one (Armed Forces Expeditionary Medal).

When all of this was over, I was ready to get back to the West Coast to get married and go to a class "C" school for a new weapon system. I did this by reenlisting early before the original contract expired and received some bonus money. I was heading to Mare Island Naval shipyard in Vallejo, California. The training was for my conversion to missiles. I was a Gunfire Control Technician and was going to become a Missile Fire Control Technician. At this same time our insignias would change. Back when I was struggling in the basic electricity tracks of school, I was there for so long that I had managed to become part of the collection of students in the fire control technician class that would design the new shoulder patch rating insignia. So many of us had lightning bolts around the rangefinder as a result of an electrical charge, that it became the official icon on the rating patch.

Chapter 21

Marriage is as Green as a Fresh Spring Layer of Grass

I had another experience stationed on board the USS Biddle CG-34; I fell in love with a girl all the way back home. I was as green as a fresh spring layer of grass. However, I had no clue what love was or meant. Between Great Lakes and Virginia, I went for a brief two-week vacation before reporting to the ship in late 1983. I went home to Los Angeles and stayed with my parents and my brother Michael, sister Heather, and my mother's little dog. My brother, Steve was still out not contributing to the family or household. Read his book, and he will tell you what he was doing. My older sister, Verna was buying another property or already owned it. My dad and I had a brief discussion about getting a life insurance policy and how the family was bonded economically. My eldest brother Michael carried everyone's financial load. My brother Steven's addictions were causing him to always be in need of money, and that made me distrustful of conducting business with him. I would receive reports from my mother and father about how Steven's demons caused him to bust console televisions. He even broke the huge front window pane, which cost Michael thousands of dollars. Standing in the family home, Michael told me about helping him with a townhome development on the lot. The land was tied up between Steven, Verna, and Michael, with only Michael holding the bag financially, and my mother and father doing what they do best, what they have always done as long as I've known them. My parents were great managers and organizers with all of our belongings over the years. They also controlled and guided most of our decisions. Needless to say, the property owned by my older siblings was under total control of my parents. They managed and kept up the property at 1327 Van Ness Avenue Los Angeles, CA. I never lived there for an extended period, but it was home because I could not call anyplace else home.

I got together with my best friend from Los Angeles High School, Kirk Kemp. We went to a nightclub in Los Angeles named the Carolina West. I had never been to a club like that. I was 21 years old. There were beautiful women everywhere. My buddy Kirk had already been into this side of life. I was the late bloomer. I was all over the place in that nightclub. The dance floor was made up like streets and street signs and curbs and sidewalks. There were also telephones at the tables so that I could call someone's table to ask for a dance. I thought that was great because if she said no, I could avoid the long walk back to the table alone.

I met Anita L. Rogers at the Carolina West. She was with her girlfriend. We played on those phones. We pretended to be dating already. She really loved to talk, so this setup was perfect for her. I learned so much about her. She had a daughter named Keniece. This was an entirely new and, at times, overwhelming relationship. I'd never been in a real relationship. I was star-struck. It would upset my father because it meant I was not going to let him control any of my future, especially when it came to love. I was 21, and there was no structural family relationship that most are accustomed to. I was rebellious momentarily. I don't remember how things went so fast, but I was engaged to a woman with a child by the time I got on a flight going back to Virginia. The last discussion my father and I had involved a concern any father should have. I was reluctant to listen because of my stubbornness. I realize now, the words he was trying to tell me made sense. "Take your time and don't do things out of haste.... Son, if you are coming home to a woman this suddenly with your bags and staying there, then that is not just dating." He went on to say, "That situation will be problematic. How do you know some other man is not leaving his bags there for the weekend?" This thought he put in my head would last forever and enter my mind whenever I was dating or in any relationship.

We were upset. Anita was really mad. It took her a long time to like him. She began to understand that I did not know them that well myself. My fiancée and I would make two attempts toward marriage while we ignored our very first warning sign not to go through with it. The first attempt to get married was when I had just purchased my candy apple red 280z from my buddy Kirk. It was a clean, 1975 classic piece of eye-candy that the police loved to see coming. My wife-to-be and I were heading to Las Vegas to tie the knot with the Justice of the Peace. We decided we did not need a big honeymoon or expensive wedding because, as she said: "I cannot wear white anyway because I have a daughter." Needless to say, on our way to the event, the 280z broke down outside of Barstow, California. A warning sign like no other. Something greater than myself and my father was trying to say, "Do not do this; it is not for the two of you." Like any other dumb, determined, sexually-fueled and economically-deprived youth, I only visualized the dollar signs of the union growing to a bigger purse. Within about six months and a $700 head gasket job on the engine valves, we were married. The central conflicts in our marriage were mainly about how to communicate and how money was spent. How do we save money? How could I control my envy through communication? I was insecure about trusting, even after the purchase of a home and the birth of a new baby. Yes, a new baby.

Chapter 22

Greatest Ship Ever, USS England CG-22

A new ship. A new identity. I was now a Second-Class Petty Officer, married with a baby on the way. I accomplished getting advanced to second class, and I was officially a 3-D 48C Air Search Radar Technician. I was not long onboard before I was making my first WESTPAC when the ship that I was attached to was ready to go on a six-month deployment at sea. While serving onboard the USS Biddle CG-34, I had already made a 3-month deployment through the North Atlantic Ocean and the Black Sea Region. Following that, I made the Mediterranean Sea and Indian Ocean cruise for six-months onboard USS Biddle CG-34.

Now onboard the USS England, I had a little seniority. I was a seasoned sailor, not just some rick-recruit. When I made acquaintances this time around, it was more of a team member welcoming. Although I could feel hints of competitiveness, it did not surface right away. The next few years, things went as well as could be expected in Navy life. I became an Enlisted Surface Warfare Specialist onboard. I had to take the oral exam twice. The officers wanted to pass me, but they needed me to really understand how everything on the ship worked and how to jump in a position anywhere on the ship and lend assistance. The second time on the oral board, I made it. Now I was an Enlisted Surface Warfare Specialist (ESWS), Fire Controlman Second Class Petty Officer (FC2). Makes my chest stick out just typing all that. Time for West Pacific Cruise (WESTPAC). Brittany was not born yet, but things were already on the skids between Anita and me because of deployments and money woes.

A child and wife: my family. I was not the most fabulous husband but willing to learn to be one. I became a great dad later, after parenting classes and nearly receiving a domestic violence criminal record if I did not change my ways. I did some step-fathering with Keniece my step-daughter. We are father and daughter today, and she has children – my step-grandchildren.

I had always heard stories about the Orient and making a WESTPAC across the equator and becoming a Shellback on our way to Australia. Anyone who has not passed the equator onboard the ship is a Polliwog. A Polliwog is the lowest specimen of a creature or human to ever consider themselves a sailor. In other words, according to the mythical Captain Neptune, the Captain of a ship all the way down to the lowliest sailor is a Polliwog. A Polliwog becomes a Shellback by crossing to the south of the equator onboard a Naval vessel.

An infrequent occasion deserves a very special initiation. During the 24 hours while the ship is crossing the equator, the Shellbacks put all the Pollywogs through the garbage, and made to dress as drag-queens or filthy ship-hands, wallowing in trash and slime and torture, all in fun. I must say the Shellback queens looked like beautiful women. Remember, guys are already at sea for a while before this ritual. We voted on who was the prettiest wench to give to the sea and the ghost of Captain Neptune while crossing the equator. Everyone else tried their best to dress like some kind of a swashbuckling sailor. We were run through man-made garbage obstacle courses while getting beaten with a shillelagh, a pirate whooping tool, and humiliated for fun throughout the day. In the end, we were all Shellbacks and on our way to Australia for sun, fun, port, and liberty.

We also went to Japan, Korea, the Philippines, and, on the way back, to the Philippines again and Hawaii. We completed one more mission before I reenlisted onboard the USS England CG-22. Many times, in the Navy, it was about being in the right place at the right time. We were detoured coming back to lend support for the invasion of Panama and the capture of Manuel Noriega. Mission Accomplished, and medals for participation received. One more plus about the USS England CG-22 was the comradery. This ship matched personalities and age brackets on the ship, including officers and enlisted sailors. I loved this ship the most. I had a great sleeping situation: middle rack, the premiere of enlisted shipboard living. I had space and convenience.

I met another black guy while serving onboard the USS England who was a few years younger. I became kind of a mentor and ally. Lieutenant Avery Penn. I was proud of him because he was able to succeed. I knew he could because when I first met him, he had the foundation that I never received – a normal childhood experience, complete with social acceptance and education beyond what was expected for the next wave of black men in the Fire Control Program. When we met, we were the only two black Fire Controlmen onboard. He worked on the phalanx gauntlet gun, an anti-air weapon that could shoot off three-thousand rounds a minute. We were both second class. We also understood, and sometimes discussed, how to handle indifference we would occasionally encounter. They all knew Avery, and I would protect him. I had now been on the following: A North Atlantic cruise, a Mediterranean, Indian Ocean, and a WESTPAC. Time to leave the USS England CG-22 as an Enlisted Surface Warfare Specialist Petty Officer First Class Fire Controlman on his way to shore-duty for a land-based teaching and maintenance assignment.

I landed this shore duty assignment at Point Loma, San Diego. It was a three-year appointment that allowed me to have family time, live at home, and have a workday that looked more like a regular job. This set-up weighed heavily on the marriage. I had two different Leading Petty Officers stationed here from whom I acquired most of my training as a newly promoted Fire Control First Class Petty Officer. On my first day, I sat down to meet Petty Officer Feutz and he said to me, "When I'm in Alabama, I'm a good old boy, but while we are stationed together I will treat you fairly." I responded, "I guess I can't expect more." Time passed, and when Benjamin Feutz was leaving, First-Class Petty Officer Brad Cardwell was reporting with a few months' overlapping. He had squared away. He was an extremely knowledgeable electronics technician. I had never worked with a person who had both a polished understanding of the Navy Code of Military Justice and refined skills as a Fire Controlman. I had never encountered a work ethic like his, and he was persistent and made our assignment an integral part of the wheel, beginning with our radar. The AN/SPS 48C Three D Air Search Radar was the eyes and ears of the fire control system and the entire ship itself. I understood this before I ever went to systems school. I felt like a significant cog in the wheel.

What he taught was how to enjoy hard work and staying busy to help the day move along faster. We were all part of the mission. He also recognized who and what type of human Ben Feutz was. Everyone in the military needs a person like Chief Brad Cardwell. He tried to get me prepared for Chief Petty Officer. I learned so much. I earned my Navy Achievement Medal under him. The radar at Point Loma during our tenure could have been mounted on any ship and become an integral piece of equipment on board that vessel.

Unfortunately, this would also be where my marriage started to crumble. Chief Cardwell knew about me, where I had come from, and how illiteracy was affecting my life. He knew more about me and the cruelty I faced than I could ever get my wife to understand. So many things about my life and who I was I could not understand or explain to people. It always turned into crazy talk because no one could comprehend why this had not happened to anyone else. I've been wandering through life with the crazy tag, but now I can explain it as an injustice. I don't share the enthusiasm for life, liberty, and the pursuit of happiness anymore. I re-enlisted for money and debt relief. Marriage was costly. Divorce cost more. I left Chief Cardwell having a Naval Achievement medal and the highest recommendation for Chief Petty Officer anyone could have received from anyone. All I had to do was pass a test. I had two more schools under my belt now. I went to Tomahawk school to master the long range, anti-anything missile. I also headed to Mare Island in Vallejo, California.

Chapter 23

What? You're TUPAC's EX?

I was sitting alone in my newly rented apartment. I had a chair, my duffle bag, and the 13-inch barracks television that I purchased back when I first got divorced. I had been there so many times in my life, sitting alone and thinking. I had no clue how to get things going. I had never been taught or knew what type of dedication or conviction was necessary to participate or become a part of a civilian career scheme. The learning curve in life took off there. I always had guaranteed income or no worry about it. I did have about $25,000, not a lot of money without the prospect of work. I put it away because it was going to sit in the bank until I could figure out what to do. I thought this was a good plan. I had a couple of buddies who also got out around the same time. We were doing the usual, looking for work by day and party, party, party in the evening.

Mare Island, Vallejo, California was where I first attended AN/SPS 48C Radar training between the tour of the USS Biddle CG-34 and before checking onboard the USS England CG-22. I was leaving shore duty and attending 55B Terrier Guided Missile Radar School. Then, I was to continue to Terrier Guided Missile

Control Systems School. Some things happened while attending school there this time around that provided an education on a different level.

On one occasion while I was divorced, I was sitting at a bar with my ex-wife's dad. We bought each other a drink and shared some small talk about the grandkids and we settled any animosity between us. I was also able to do that with my ex-wife's mother, the kind and beautiful Betty Herron (RIP). I realized that black folks had so many things going on in our own lives that were complicated, it was tough to empathize with anyone else.

Another scenario that led to an epiphany was a result of how tight the First Classes, Chiefs, and Senior Chiefs were. It was the ultimate in political schmoozing and hobnobbing. One of the black guys who was a friend and classmate was a Chief. I went to a base trial as a witness to testify about an altercation he had at a base dance club. Otherwise, nobody was engaging me as part of their schmoozing. I honestly knew that they would rather not have me around. My experience was that nerds who were not discussing electronics were discussing people. I decided to just attend school and explore Northern California.

I met several girls. I really enjoyed the Highway 101 area – Cotati, Daily City, Rohnert Park – up along the coast. I was dating and very good friends with the beautiful Ms. Tomeka Jones. I was in the nightclub partying with some buddies as usual. The "Daily Planet" was the local spot in Rohnert Park. This beautiful lady in a red dress with fantastic curves came toward me and asked me to dance. The rest is history. One day after dating a couple of weeks, we were sitting in the car in Rohnert Park and walking towards the car was the not-yet-discovered Tupac Shakur, two nights before performing at a club called Silks in Oakland with Digital Underground. It just so happened that Tomeka used to date him. The three of us were talking, shaking hands, and talking trash, and out of nowhere, he invited me to his show. He even asked me if I wanted to be a hype man and I explained to him my Navy obligations, but I went with a couple of the young dorm guys. (I was divorced and broke, attending school, reduced to living in the barracks after divorce.) Most places I travel now, people ask me what I thought about that show. It was spectacular. They were rapping and getting up on tables and dancing, all over the establishment. I was thankful to meet him and bring some friends to the show.

I took Barry Bell to that show. Barry was a young Fire Controlman Third Class that I took under my wing. He and his young buddies could at least come and talk to me if things were getting too heavy, especially when it involved race. One day in class, I got a call from Washington, DC. They called because this billet (a specific job that requires a particular rating, in this case, Fire Control First Class) that they wanted to assign me to was hard to fill. Supposedly there were reports of racial problems onboard this ship. Two things were being requested of me. The first was that I serve on the USS Long Beach CGN-9, a ship with a racial problem. I wanted to make Chief, so I couldn't say no. The second issue was that I would not be the Systems Expert that I was being trained to be, in order to position myself for Chief. So it was a request that had no benefit to me. I reported to the ship as the Leading Petty Officer and AN/SPS 48C Air Search Radar Technician. Back to the same job I had on the USS England CG-22 and at Point Loma shore duty. I was too naïve to read the signs.

When I reported to the USS Long Beach CGN-9, I saw one of the most disorganized vessels: messy, old, dirty, bad attitudes everywhere, envy, hints of racial fatigue coming from every voice. It was a mess. It made me a mess. I could not penetrate this batch of anger. Even the Chief and the Senior Chief, a 48C Tech like myself, were super passive-aggressive. I was an island and the only thing above was water. I had over forty people to manage and schedule and had to learn the new ship, while people had to get used to a new black LPO within three days of reporting. This would be the end of my Navy career. My office was up in 48C radar, the highest point on the ship, several flights from the main ship operating area. The equipment was totally disconnected, plus the antenna and gyro (a mechanism which stabilizes the antenna for balance and accuracy) was destroyed. There was a shipyard job order to replace the 48C radar antenna, a huge job. That was the main reason I was there; it was not to solve or sooth the disenfranchisement inside of that division. By the time the USS Long Beach CGN-9 was in Bremerton, Washington, I had been to a CPO review board. A Chief Petty Officer review board is for reprimands. I was reprimanded for confiscating toys like a little football and space invader video games that were continuously left out. Chief Cardwell had done the same thing before when I was being trained to lead. I was able to talk with Third Class Barry Bell on board, about most situations, but he knew I was having problems with leading as well. I also remember that the guys did not have a problem with me as long as I was just one of the crew. I really had never been taught how to handle young white men with witty mouths. I really felt that I was being undermined by those who had a problem with a black guy in charge. My chances for Chief were over. I took the early exit offer and landed here in Seattle, Washington.

Chapter 24

Out of the Navy

I was sitting alone in my newly rented apartment. I had a chair, my duffle bag, and the 13-inch barracks television that I purchased back when I first got divorced. I had been there so many times in my life, sitting alone and thinking. I had no clue how to get things going. I had never been taught or knew what type of dedication or conviction was necessary to participate or become a part of a civilian career scheme. The learning curve in life took off there. I always had guaranteed income or no worry about it. I did have about $25,000 saved, not a lot of money without the prospect of work. I put it away because it was going to sit in the bank until I could figure out what to do. I thought this was a good plan. I had a couple of buddies who also got out around the same time. We were doing the usual, looking for work by day and then it was party, party, party in the evening.

In the early days, the happy hour establishment had free food as long as you bought a drink. I usually ate places Monday through Thursday for free. I was discharged on August 29, 1992, with an honorable discharge and a record and credentials that walked on water. I really thought that work was the least of my worries. A month passed and not a bite. I was drawing unemployment when I received a phone call from my ex-wife who said, "Darryl, I cannot handle your daughter Brittany because I'm having a nervous breakdown."

My hunt for work became more aggressive because I was going to become a single dad in two months. I prepared myself for the challenge. Things were moving fast then. I landed a sub-contracting gig, which only re-adjusted my under-employment. There was no medical or dental insurance. Absolutely no benefits. Job search after job search came up empty. My very first official girlfriend in Seattle was a kind and understanding person who really loved and treated my daughter very kindly even through our break-up. I also credit her with helping me land my first job with the Washington State Department of Liquor Control Board. I was a clerk part-time. The work easiest to find was part-time or day labor. I began to see that all those shiny evaluations, recommendations, letters of appreciation, and pretty ribbons displayed across my chess like ornaments on a Christmas tree had lost value faster than a beat-up Chevy on a used car lot. I realized the error of my ways. I was too regimental. I was also very insecure. When I did not feel like I could take care of myself, I could not take care of anyone else appropriately. I felt inferior around others. My self-worth was dropping. I became suspicious of other men, similar to my marriage. I began to see that with my girlfriend and with my daughter. It destroyed the relationship. Unfortunately, we broke up, but it gave Brittany and me a chance to become closer and learn to work together. We were tight buddies, and I was also a respectable father to her.

I'd been living under the radar for a long time, drawing the least amount of attention to myself as possible. Why did I fool myself with this impossibility? All my life I had been under a microscope, every place that I had been, all the institutions that took me in, all of the foster homes that I passed through, to not see any positive result come out of our parents' battle. I've spent my life living as a political prisoner, which began for me, during the Civil Rights Movement. The courts were so enamored with this ordeal that our community of blacks and whites and every other immigrant who came to this country during my lifetime knew of me or children like me. I needed a clean slate, but a clean slate would never happen. My past was never sealed. It followed me. I was a juvenile in the system – a system categorized by color. This was my label, my tag. The distance between a black man and jail is one breath. I needed a place to catch up and see what was happening around me. I needed to separate from a society that would not provide me with answers of who I was and how this could happen. I was invisible.

The "Seattle freeze" is what people coined it here. I soon realized that being in a sanctuary city was part of the package. People in Seattle like to pretend a problem does not exist, for example, the homeless encampments under all the highways and byways in the city. This has gone on for over 20 years. Vagrancy was the first made-up charge placed on my parents, which was the initial spur of the moment "law" that allowed Los Angeles to arrest my family at a Methodist church since trespassing on public taxpayer property could not stick as a crime.

I thought that I was far enough away from Los Angeles but close enough to family that I could respond to any ordeal. If my family had any problem and needed my assistance, I felt I was close enough to hop on a plane to go and assist them. I did not need to. As time slowly progressed, I found out that family is a figment of my imagination and everything in my black world is just an illusion of what's left over from the rest of society. Or, so I thought. In general everyday conversation with folks, when sports is the topic, things were cool. I find that in most places I've traveled, as we evolve, our discussions go beyond sports. I knew by 30 what lead to the ridicule and abuse and disconnect I had experienced as a Lofton 6 family member.

Unfortunately, I have found more dilemmas in my journey through life. Within the ever-increasing tension in today's society, I find that I am in the position to pass down information that may be valuable to those like me. What I am providing is a road map of what not to do or to do it better. It wasn't so long ago that we Americans spent eight years with America's first black President of the United States, and if nothing else, we saw a country acknowledge its own multiculturalism. Even black folks had to realize other groups have formed communities in our society. During the three administrations prior to President Obama, something came to light around the country. Black men were dying by the gun at a rapid rate. The police were using deadly force more frequently. In the media around the country, the mass moral panic became black men being gunned down by police. To counter that notion, another piece of red meat was tossed out there, that there are increasing numbers of black-on-black killing. Then out comes the line, "Just look at Chicago."

I am often asked, "Why do you care? Why do you feel the need to tell your story?" My answer is, "Because the next generation may have to encounter these issues. History has a way of repeating itself." Here are a few brief episodes as I traveled through life as a disenfranchised black American male who has so far escaped becoming a statistic. Once I realized that congregating (Black men gathered together) and visibility (too much profiling by police) became red flags for me as an adult black male, I became a loner. I would tell some of my closest friends that it was my way of survival to exist under the radar. I tried doing just that. The color of my skin made it utterly impossible. Issues found me. Unavoidable issues.

Chapter 25

United States Postal Service (USPS)

I could not avoid the unavoidable issue that came up while working for the Post Office. My knees had finally gotten the best of me. The left knee went down first on a delivery route as a letter carrier. I submitted explanations. It was accepted at first. Things began happening very fast. I filed all of the proper forms. I even had the VA involved because the VA and the USPS wanted forms simultaneously. I was awaiting approval for surgery. I had immediately been transferred from the Westwood Village Post Office to the Ballard Post Office. I was assigned a limited duty desk job to wait for approval for surgery. I was called into the office by the Station Manager at Ballard, Mrs. Marsha Valdivia. She handed me a form to sign to relinquish my job title and pay scale for a part-time clerk position at lower pay and temporary job status. I asked her if I could call the union. The union said that I needed to sign in protest because this was wrong. I stated this to the station manager, and she said, "If you do not sign this then I cannot schedule you for work."

I was also scheduled for surgery. After that surgery on Monday and for the next three months, my pay was cut off, and I was "wrongfully terminated." I had no money and no job. The union seemed powerless. I hired an attorney. The first obstacle of the ordeal: finding an attorney to go up against the government for a black man. No matter how right you are, even if the law is on your side, it shows its evils.

William B. Knowles, attorney-at-law, was able to negotiate my position back, and they wanted to ignore the fact that this happened, but nothing was over. When I went back to the limited duty position continue employment while in rehab, the atmosphere was not welcoming. I was instructed by my attorney to record everything because this was not over. I found myself filling EEOC claims on discrimination of race, disability, and things that were categorized as impossible to explain. I was assigned to throw away bulk mail. The Ballard station threw out a lot of mail. Deliverable mail. I was going to be assigned with this task. I was regularly required to watch my back because the union did not know how to buffer this deliberate action on employees. This mental and emotional harassment and job assignment were my new duties as a permanent letter carrier. A rehab desk job. The USPS still had a problem with this.

It was the slap on the back of the neck heard around Seattle. I landed a job with the United States Postal Service in December 1993. I completed probation by February 1994. I was disability-retired in 2001 from the United States Post Office and Social Security Administration. I was assaulted on the job. The frustration of the long ordeal was mutually wearing on the staff of the USPS and me.

Under the management of Sam Bateman as station manager and the supervisor, Keith Reid, the USPS delivered an ultimate blow to cause a situation. I would never have imagined this could happen; it caught me entirely by surprise. Had I not been on some of the prescribed medication I was taking, I probably would have reacted differently. The reason I was taking medication was because the USPS and the VA thought that I needed it to calm myself. I remained calm enough to understand what action to take.

On that day, Supervisor Reid was arranging those huge carts that rolled around on wheels and stood about 6 feet in height. These carts are used by the clerks and staff to move large quantities of mail around the workroom floor. I did not really pay much attention to him moving these carts around. It really just seemed an ordinary day. Well...when he was done, all of the movement came to a stop. I was at my desk doing my job filling out cards. The next thing I remember was a big whack on the back of the neck. I wanted to jump right up and commence a beating. I had to stop and grit my teeth, and look around to really understand what was happening. This was the actual moment that I realized just what had been done with those carts. They had been positioned to block any view. No other employee could say they witnessed what happened. I swallowed my pride, and told supervisor Keith Reed to keep his hands off of me. I could not react out of haste, and I needed to stay calm, and one thing for sure, I had to file this assault with EEOC to have it on record. I submitted the last EEOC claim at Ballard station and then I was transferred to Columbia station. I was on some anti-depression meds. I was labeled as "disgruntled" and a number of other trumped-up adjectives.

Nothing was changing, and I needed more surgery. The interior damage was extensive in my left knee. The frustration of my situation was not making the Columbia workplace comfortable for others. I was viewed as the textbook definition of a "disgruntled employee" on the verge of "going postal." I left Columbia station to go have total left knee replacement in 1999. Nothing was going on with my claims. Then my EEOC hearing came up, and I did not win race, color, or age discrimination charges, but I did win the claim of discrimination against my disability. I was awarded minimal damages of $25,000. Despite the award for damages, the damage has not yet ended. My life has been totally altered. I was continuously facing labeling and shaming in public venues, I was being followed inside of stores, and my phones were tapped. Once, I picked up a phone in my home and the eavesdropper must have been waiting so long to listen in on my conversation that I could hear snoring on the other end. My voices startled him, and he disconnected the line immediately.

I met with my attorney, to discuss this ordeal which, by then, had been going on for several years. I was beginning to feel weary and distraught. Life was starting to become meaningless too. I owned a couple of guns. I stated to my attorney that I did not feel that I was supposed to be here anymore. I really felt that this was not the time for me or someone who looked like me to be on the planet. I contemplated putting a gun in my mouth and blowing my brains out. I really came close. I must have loaded and unloaded my two clips about seven times one evening. I was thinking to myself that if the bullets were not in the clip, then I definitely won't off myself. I refused to admit that I was crazy. So, I told my attorney that and he said that there is a way to prove to them that you are not the crazy person. He asked me to check into the VA psych ward and told me to explain it all to them. He said this is one of the best ways to prove that you are not crazy. I fell hard for that one. He was only getting rid of me and double-crossed me. But for what reason?

Shortly after that, I learned my attorney had been charged with criminal charges for child sex trafficking. Great! It took forever to find a lawyer who would even look at my case, and now he was gone. I was checked out of the VA psych ward on antipsychotic and extreme depression meds. While on the seventh-floor psych ward, my home was burglarized. I was not aware of all my losses immediately because of the meds. The Post Office retired me, but it was unofficial because Social Security also has to retire you, as well. I was in this low-income, weird disability situation where I didn't really have a job, but I was getting a small income to stay afloat. The VA was up to about 50% of disability, meaning my pay scale went up. Percentage of bodily loss is how compensation pay is calculated There were income assistance places throughout the city where I could get some temporary help. The food banks would help to sustain the grocery bill. I learned how to live on the bare essentials because, labeled and shamed, no one would hire me. No one wanted to be around me. My friends became the homeless and disenfranchised from most of the darkest places in Seattle. They were of all ethnicities. I believe these associations were the reason the police put me on their radar. It's just an assumption. I have been going through this for far too long to ignore how things work.

Chapter 26

The Final Frontier of a Losing Streak

I began paying more attention to my health: eating right, exercising, and getting ample sleep. I started walking in a local park on a regular basis at different times. On my walks, I would be friendly and greet folks in return because it was essential to ease public perception of a black man exercising in public. Some people called the shyness of the public as the "Seattle Freeze," but I've learned that it is best to remain as under the radar as possible. On occasion, I would say hello to a group of fellas of various ethnicities on my walks, and on one of those days, I chose to stop and shoot the breeze. Not more than twenty feet away was an open container of beer. An officer walked up and asked, "Is that one of your containers?" and I told him it wasn't. A simple act of shooting the breeze with a group of men, and that moment of my walk turned five minutes into forty minutes because, as a black man in the group, the open container 20 feet away *had* to be mine. My driver's license, the only one requested by the police, was eventually returned.

The next issue relates to the four police officers gunned down while drinking coffee at Starbucks in Tacoma. There was significant tension in Seattle during the end of the '90s and through the 2000s because of the War on Drugs, black people congregating, crack cocaine, and the justice system. Due process and equal protection was a routine struggle. During this period, the police department had a lot of money. Overtime and protection became very profitable for law enforcement. I had a personal encounter with two of those officers. A new YMCA had opened in SeaTac, Washington. Gentrification was in full effect. The Central District in Seattle had already been gutted. I was trying to continue my path of living under the radar. I joined the YMCA and was a semi-regular. Folks who know me know that the gym is a big part of my life. On a few occasions, I would hear this random group of officers speaking and joking about their arrests and busts. I paid minor attention to it and kept to my business. It did not matter. I was only to be a member for a couple of months. One of the officers, whom I thought was a nice guy and said hello from time to time, began to talk to me and wanted to find out more of who I was. He asked, "What part of town do you live in?" I said, "White Center, but I am just trying out a new gym." Within a week, a couple of those officers had the front office feeling that I made people uncomfortable at the gym. People began staring at me when I came from then on.

Eventually the YMCA would have the black maintenance guy come and tell me that the organization felt that I made people there uncomfortable and that they were terminating my membership. Looking back at this, I wish I would have resorted to civil disobedience and staged a sit-in. Once again, I claimed the path of swallowing my pride. A couple of months later, I was reading the newspaper, and they showed pictures of the four officers gunned down in Starbucks, and two of them were the ones who had me thrown out of the YMCA. The perpetrator was caught and killed. It was said that he was a hired gun flown all the way from Mississippi to do the hit. I only want to provide an idea of how we were corralled or restricted in where and when black men could go peacefully. The police, I found out later, were privy to overtime and protection money from public and private businesses. If the proprietor wanted black men harassed and removed, police were the muscle.

This next form of abuse came totally from the "illustrious steam room troll," someone hanging out in the areas of the gym where conversations are relaxed and casual. They are almost like an internet troll. They gather pertinent information about you. This ordeal involved the law firm/collection agency Suttle and Associates, Capital One, Grange Auto Insurance, Millennium Ford in Burien, WA, and the Burien Police Department. I took my Ford Bronco in for some work. I finally had just paid it off so I could afford to make some repairs. I only expected the job to be completed by the end of the day at Millennium Ford. They needed to finish work, and it would need to stay another day. By the next day, Millennium Ford called and said my vehicle had been stolen from their shop. I recalled them asking if I had another car, but I knew what they were getting at and told them I did not need a loaner because I had no plans that evening. What they did not know was that I had another car in my driveway; a raggedy mini-van RV that I drove down to Millennium Ford to fill out the police report. Was it coincidental that the Social Security Administration was in Burien?

There the police did their job, or at least it appeared. The car remained missing for up to 30 days, the deadline for claiming a totaled or missing vehicle. When the vehicle was found, it had

Ford vehicle keys all over the floor and over 20,000 more miles on it. Ripped and sliced plastic was everywhere, the plastic coated with the residue of white powder that numbed your tongue. It appeared that the Bronco had been part of some drug transport vehicle and then returned to me. Everything went utterly wrong after this. The Burien Police Department did not want to look into the matter any further. Millennium Ford overcharged me $3,600 and gave me a $200 discount for my troubles, and I still owed Capitol One $3,400 and whatever else was on the credit card. I wrote Capitol one and complained I wanted some kind of recovery for damages. I discussed the matter with Capital One and with Grange Insurance. I was meeting dead ends trying to talk sense to them. I was not paying until this matter got resolved. Wrong answer. Capital One sent me to collections for around $3,800. Grange Insurance canceled and billed me. The sauna room troll turned out to be a collecting agent for Suttle and Associates. I had to actually hunt that collection company down. It was playing hide-the-salami. Moving about western Washington, delaying any connection, and $3,400 turns into $6,200 with interest and a few years of hide and seek.

Finally, I worked out a deal to make payments because I was catching hell in every other aspect of my life. This debt situation happened between 2005 – 2011, right in the middle of the great housing fiasco. I was locked into a 7% interest rate, and I could not refinance because banks were freezing money and taking homes from poor people with this government "lower your interest rate scam." The bank representatives told me that for this to work, I had to stop making payments on my home so that I could go into debt. This would force the government to provide me with a lower interest loan. I did not do that because I had heard that people were actually losing their homes due to that process. It was 2010, and I was within about $700 left on collection debt, and the Suttle and Associates Office could not be found. So, I staked out a UPS driver in Bellevue, Washington, and found out through him where their office was. The UPS driver said that the company relocated often. I arrived in the office a little frustrated, but composed. I was in the waiting area, and there were no chairs there. There was only a glass window with a slot for exchanging items. There was a desk and phone with a speaker on it looking through the glass. No one was sitting there. I paced for several minutes. I knew they had to be watching me. This waiting room could have held a WWF match in it because there was nothing to get busted up.

The sauna room troll came out with a bodyguard. We began discussing the debt in the waiting area. He stepped closer to me. When I said that I would like to end this debt and close this account, the bodyguard stepped even closer to me and raised his hands and arms as if in preparation to grab ahold of me. The boss troll lifted his back of right hand signaling to the bouncer to stop in his tracks. The bouncer stopped. At that moment, I was in a standing prayer stance with my slightly closed eyes facing down in preparation for the physical shock I was about to endure. It did not happen. The Bouncer backed away. The troll asked me if that was what I wanted and we shook hands on it. It would take a couple more reminder visits to get the judgment signed and closed. By 2011, I was finally able to obtain a 3.75 interest rate for 15 years. I was now ready to clean up the next phase of life and to be accepted into a master's program at Seattle University. Honestly, which program did not matter. I just needed to get in to catch up with time lost. My undergraduate degree pointed toward criminal justice. I knew I did not want to be a police officer, and given my age, I knew they did not want me. I was informed that there were many other directions that you can take in criminal justice, so I applied and sold myself. My Master's in Criminal Justice, Investigation Track ended with a completed 3.1 GPA. I am awaiting my second comp test. I prefer writing this book.

Before the Seattle University master's program, I needed to complete my undergraduate degree. Before 2001 when my disability retirement was finalized, I was attending Central Washington University in pursuit of an undergraduate degree. I had been working on this since 1979 when I first enrolled at Cal State-Northridge. I accumulated my credits and schooling throughout the military and all the junior colleges that I had attended, including South Seattle Community College, and received my AA degree.

In 2001, Central Washington University assigned a counselor to me. She would question me on 300 and 400 level classes, and give me assignments I was to take home and complete. They were setting me up to fail. The head of the criminal justice policing program did not want me in the program. Why? This was another example of the bureaucracies joining together to drive me out. Feeling isolated again, I used essay question assignments to explain the injustices I had been experiencing. I could only tie this act to my parents' lawsuit, case #895188. But I finally got a degree, which should have been a red flag. I later found out the degree from this school wasn't very meaningful and ensured that no organization would ever hire me.

I was checked into the seventh floor of the VA hospital, supposedly to prove my sanity, at the request of the same attorney who had been working on my previous wrongful termination case with the United States Postal Service. I saved the article about my attorney getting sentenced to five years in prison and losing his license to practice law. I believed that he was in agreement with me that I was being harassed and targeted for my EEOC claims and limited duty status. When I was released after nine days from the psych ward, I was out there. I was going to anti-psychotic counseling and depression classes. I was also on medication until I quit taking it in 2005. In all my life, I had never endured this amount of labeling and shaming, leading to a life where I just wanted to remain hidden and under the radar.

It was 2011, and I was disability retired. I had paid my debt in full. I'd established a relationship with a better understanding of my life with my two kids. I had a bachelor's degree from the diploma mill, Central Washington University. I was a *Crime Scene Investigator*. During that time, I was trying to think of a master's program that I could stimulate an interest in and pursue. I needed something that was tailored to my undergraduate degree, or I would not be accepted. I tried the LSAT twice and just could not get by all the inferences. Failed it twice. I began looking into Criminal Justice. All of my experience up to this point involved dealing with law, crime, disenfranchisement, poverty, and oppression. I found myself becoming an outcast and feeling I was being labeled a lone wolf. I was feeling extremely ostracized at this point in my life. I was able to clean up as much as I could to increase the odds of being accepted into Seattle University's Criminal Justice Master's Program. By 2014, I had a 3.1 GPA. I had just failed the comprehensive exam which can be taken twice, but my left knee was killing me. I had one more chance to take it. But

I also had to go in for a third surgery on my left knee, which would be a total knee replacement. It had gotten so bad, I also had lymphedema (swelling in the lower extremities where you need to wear compression stockings for circulation), in both legs. It was at Seattle University that I saw how much of an outlier I really was. This time it was mostly due to my age. I was determined to do my best despite all of this. My psychological battles were many; I was heading in a path that might not be for me.

It was during a presentation with the Seattle Police Department that I realized I needed to change some of the things I was doing in my life. I was sitting near Assistant Chief Stanton and I knew that guilt by association with some guys was going to eventually catch up to me. I was motivated to go back to school to attain my Master's degree, knowing it would help me clean up my reputation and my life.

I completed all my classes, but after surgery, I had new battles to fight. My age was an issue. Interest, motivation, and determination weren't what they once were. I had new bills facing me. One was more than $10,000 charged by three attorneys due to a non-easement issue with my neighbors. The City of Seattle made me purchase a new sewer in 1995 but a pipe I was unaware of allowed my neighbors to tap into my sewer without a legal easement agreement. Because of the covert piping, I didn't have full ownership that I should have had, but I was the one stuck with a bill for $19,600 to repair foundational damage. The sewer pipe needed to be removed or the land would be taken from me.

Justice for black males, is close to impossible in this country. Even when property damage is involved, the white person or party has the advantage. In addition to trespassing and stealing my property, my neighbor put me in an Emmett Till situation. Remember Emmett Till? He was murdered for whistling at a white woman. She put me in the same situation by accusing me of harassment, and the court assigned the case to another jurisdiction in Burien, Washington, so that the issue of the trespass would not surface in court. I was immediately swept off to a mediation where I believed my story would not matter, and it did not. This is how the system of provincialism works for white people. In mediation, I was told what a friendly neighbor I was, and there was no harassment ever mentioned. This was about the City of Seattle helping my white neighbor steal my land and sewer, and I continued paying fees to three different white attorneys who would not come up with a case to put before a judge. Unless they are affluent, black people only get plea bargains.

So even though I did all the right things – got my education, attained a degree, abided by the law – in the end none of it really changed the outcome of my lot in life.

Conclusion

Living in Washington has shown me a different perspective of the prism of race. I have learned the many aspects of diversity. The foster care system is very diverse in Seattle, Washington. I have personally met white children in black foster homes, and I have met black children in white foster homes. In those brief encounters, I can say that I witnessed happiness and joy. I have seen cross-overs in the music industry, with rap music being accepted by various cultures and people of every color dancing together. I see singers, rappers, dancers, nerds, athletes, and goths intermingling everywhere. We increasingly live in a multicultural, multiethnic, society. Why shouldn't we foster an image of that?

Many people feel that Brown v. Board of Education put an end to Separate but Equal, and then there are many who would say that things are exactly the same or even worse. I experienced the devastating and life-altering fallout with my family and countless others. My father Leon E. Lofton Jr., Master Sergeant of the US Army, passed away in 2004 and will never get the opportunity to read my research. My eldest brother Michael L. Lofton passed away February 2018, so we never finished our discussion. Rest in peace my family. I am not a bitter man. I am an American citizen. I do not feel that society really understands or realizes what we went through, sitting next to each other in a classroom and learning together.

The most challenging event in my education and what gave me the most preparation to write this book was my three-year pursuit of my master's degree at Seattle University. The course curriculum was challenging to me, but I truly believe that I placed myself in the right position and location in life to re-experience and understand what my parents experienced. During my most dreadful days of depression, I felt that my struggles were similar to my father's when he was walking and pacing the blocks of Anchorage, Alaska, begging for a ride back to California. He experienced the shaming, labeling, profiling, and targeting, which are building blocks for stop-and-frisk. I would like many to take from this journey the importance of "The Rule of Law." Understand it and live by it. Laws can only protect you, if one understands how they work. My father's instructions, during our brief times together in a vehicle, were not to make any sudden moves when an officer is approaching a vehicle. Announce all movement you intend on making in an officer's presence.

Even today, there are areas facing the racial struggles and class struggles that permeate our country. These issues involving difference (and indifference) is what makes working and living together a difficult journey. Although there has been significant progress, the story of this nation's struggle to overcome issues of race and law continues.

And the result of those struggles can lead to other more personal and irreparable struggles, with outcomes that last a lifetime. There are no Thanksgiving or Christmas gatherings for us Loftons, for we have grown apart. So, our story, for now, will end here.

Appendix A

Official court case document of docket case #895188

Below is a copy of the original Case #895188, *Leon E. Lofton Jr. And Esther M. Lofton vs. The Los Angeles Unified School District*, filed by Leon E. Lofton Jr. and Esther M. Lofton on April 12, 1967.

PRETRIAL FORM NO. 1

N O T I C E

Pursuant to Rule 222, Rules for the Superior Court, adopted by the Judicial Council, as amended, effective September 1, 1964, Sections 1, 6, 10, 12 and 13 of this form need not now be completed if waiver of pretrial is sought.

LEON E. LOFTON, JR. AND

~~Attorney for~~ ESTHER M.H. (pro. per.)

541 W. MANCHESTER BLV'D #7, INGLEWOOD, CALIF.
Address

Telephone No. (NONE)

SUPERIOR COURT OF THE STATE OF CALIFORNIA
FOR THE COUNTY OF LOS ANGELES

LEON E. LOFTON, JR. AND
ESTHER M.H. LOFTON.

No. 895188

JOINT PRETRIAL STATEMENT

Plaintiff(s)

SCHOOL BOARD MEMBERS
OF LOS ANGELES UNIFIED
SCHOOL DISTRICT AND ALL
JOHN DOES.

Defendant(s)

Check Applicable Box:

1. ☒ Request for waiver of pretrial conference and pretrial order.[1]

2. ☐ Auto accident case.

3. ☒ General civil case.

[Before completing this form, read Pretrial Policy Memorandum and follow instructions in check list. Wherever insufficient space is provided in this form, additional sheets should be attached as exhibits.[2]]

The undersigned, being all of the parties who have appeared in this action, or their counsel, file this joint statement pursuant to Rule 210(c) [or Rule 222 (waiver)].

1. NATURE OF THE CASE:
Conspiracy to deprive Leon E., Jr. and Esther M.H. Lofton of the right to work as teachers or in any other endeavor, through:
a. Fraud
b. Political maneuvers
c. Denial of Due Process of Law
d. Unfair Judicial Decision
e. Illegal search of property (furniture)
f. Illegal seizure of property (U.S. Mails)

IF NOT AUTO ACCIDENT CASE, SET FORTH AGREED OR ADMITTED MATTERS
IN THIS SPACE (ADD SHEETS IF NECESSARY)

No matter has been denied.
- Original action was accepted with "good cause appearing
therefore" signed in Change of Venue by Judge Chas.
Johnson of Sacramento Superior Court.

— CRA6266 Appellate Department of Superior Court of Los
Angeles which contains same matters was accepted "on its
merits."

3. SETTLEMENT. We certify that the parties have, in good faith, discussed settlement but
cannot agree upon a settlement. (See L. A. Pretrial Policy Memorandum No. 10 B.)

4. DISCOVERY. We certify that all depositions and discovery proceedings have been completed, except as follows (EXPLAIN VARIANCE FROM CERTIFICATE OF READINESS):
CRA 6266 (above) and hearings in Matters of Juvenile
Court of Los Angeles (No. 10) could be classed as depositions
and discovery.

5. LAW AND MOTION. No law and motion matters are pending or contemplated, except as
follows for the following reasons (EXPLAIN VARIANCE FROM CERTIFICATE OF READI-
NESS):

6. UNSERVED PARTIES. It is requested that the action be dismissed as to all defendants/
cross-defendants, except: (Insert names of all defendants/cross-defendants to be retained in
suit.)
Mr. William Corragar, Mrs. Kathleen Stevens, Mrs. Bowman,
Mr. Paul Herberg, Mr. Art Burns; Mrs. Lucille Burkhalter,
et al.) E. M. L. & L. E. Tytan g., Los Angeles Unified School district.
AA.

The reasons for not requesting dismissal as to any unserved party who has not appeared and
who has not been defaulted are as follows:
The members of the School Board, a corporate body, are

—165—

7. **REQUEST FOR PRETRIAL WAIVER.** We certify that in our opinion neither attendance at a pretrial conference nor a pretrial order would serve a useful purpose. (If not a waiver case, say NOT APPLICABLE.)

8. **ESTIMATED TRIAL TIME AND JURY DEMAND.** The time estimated for trial is _5_ days. Jury trial has (NOT) been demanded by

Mr. Ron Apperson, Deputy County Counsel
~~plaintiff(s)~~/defendant(s)

9. **AGREEABLE TRIAL DATE.** We have contacted the calendar clerk and have been advised that the following trial date is available which is convenient to all counsel: (If not a waiver case, say NOT APPLICABLE.) We are always available, (Emil and I.I.Jr.)

10. **RELATED CASES.** The following cases are pending which arose out of the same occurrence (if "none", so state): Matters of: (JUVENILE COURT)

Michael Lofton 317592-019,985 CE 46
Verna   " 317593-019,986 CE 46
Steven   " 317594-019,957 CE 46
Darry   " 323623-0200074, CE 46
Tracy   " 323624-0200742 CE 46
Nina   " 323625-0200743 CE 46

11. **NOTICE OF TRIAL.** The parties do/~~do not~~ waive notice of trial.
(strike one)

12. **EXTENSION OF TIME TO RULE ON WAIVER.** If the court, within the time provided by Rule 222 for the court to act on this request for pretrial waiver, orders this case placed on the Special Pretrial Settlement Calendar pursuant to Rule 207.5, the time within which the court may act on this waiver request is extended to and including the 10th day after the conclusion of the settlement conference. (If not a waiver case, NOT APPLICABLE.)

13. **STATEMENT OF LEGAL AND FACTUAL CONTENTIONS.**[*] The joint or separate statement(s) of legal and factual contentions as to the issues remaining in dispute and itemization of claimed special and general damages as required by Rule 210 (c) or Rule 222 (c) (if applicable), are attached hereto or will be filed separately.

14. **PROPOSED ORDER.**[*] A proposed order waiving pretrial conference and pretrial order is filed herewith. (If not a waiver case, say NOT APPLICABLE.)

DATED: _December 21, 1966_ , 19 _66_.

Lion E. Lofton, Jr.
Esther M. H. Lofton
~~Attorney~~(s) for Plaintiff(s)

Attorney(s) for Defendant(s)
1-23-67

[*] Use Pretrial Form No. 2 for this. All such statements must be filed within the required time. See L. A. Pretrial Pol. Memo., Par. 6(a).

[b] Use Pretrial Form No. 3.

BIBLIOGRAPHY

1. *The Hidden Dimension: An Inside View on The Reality of Inner-City African America* Paperback – May 20, 2016 by Steven Blane Lofton, Amazon Books

2. *Theft by Court: Inglewood and Culver City Municipal Courts Enforce Black Codes* by Esther M Lofton, Feb 23, 2013, Amazon Books

3. *The Brown Decision in Retrospect: Commemoration or Celebration.* The Western Journal of Black Studies, Vol. 31, Jackson, C. (2007). No. 2, 2007. p. 28-33.

ABOUT THE AUTHOR

Darryl Lofton lives in Seattle Washington. He has a daughter, a grandson, as well as a stepdaughter who also has children. He likes to say he is from Los Angeles, but that was long ago. Darryl's journey starts in Los Angeles and includes the greater-Los Angeles area and its many enclaves.

Made in the USA
Middletown, DE
23 March 2019